GLADIA✝ORS ARISING

GLADIATORS ARISING

BLOOD-BOUGHT VS. BLOOD SPORT

TRENT HERBERT

AMBASSADOR INTERNATIONAL
GREENVILLE, SOUTH CAROLINA & BELFAST, NORTHERN IRELAND

www.ambassador-international.com

Gladiators Arising

Blood-Bought vs. Blood Sport

©2022 by Trent Herbert
All rights reserved

ISBN: 978-1-62020-851-9
eISBN: 978-1-62020-883-0

Cover Design by Joshua Frederick
Interior Typesetting by Dentelle Design
Edited by Katie Cruice Smith

Unless otherwise noted, all Scripture taken from the New American Standard Bible© Copyright ©1960, 1962, 1963, 1968, 1971, 1972, 1973, 1975, 1977, 1995 by The Lockman Foundation. Used by permission. (www.Lockman.org)

Scripture marked BLB taken from The Holy Bible, Berean Literal Bible, BLB Copyright ©2016 by Bible Hub. Used by Permission. All Rights Reserved Worldwide.

AMBASSADOR INTERNATIONAL
Emerald House
411 University Ridge, Suite B14
Greenville, SC 29601
United States
www.ambassador-international.com

AMBASSADOR BOOKS
The Mount
2 Woodstock Link
Belfast, BT6 8DD
Northern Ireland, United Kingdom
www.ambassadormedia.co.uk

The colophon is a trademark of Ambassador, a Christian publishing company.

To the glory of God and His continuing epic story

TABLE OF CONTENTS

ACKNOWLEDGMENTS   9

INTRODUCTION
GLADIATORS ARISING   11

CHAPTER 1
ENTER THE RING   15

CHAPTER 2
THE VICTORY OF THE CROSS   25

CHAPTER 3
THE NEW GLADIATORS   41

CHAPTER 4
BLOOD-BOUGHT VS. BLOOD SPORT   57

CHAPTER 5
THE CONCUSSION CRISIS   69

CHAPTER 6
THE NEW ROME ARISING?   87

AFTERWORD   103

ENDNOTES   105

BIBLIOGRAPHY   125

ACKNOWLEDGMENTS

I want to thank my wife, Laurie, whom God gave to me as His precious gift to stand with me. Also, my parents, David and Irene Herbert, who spent many hours reviewing my stream of manuscript revisions.

GLADIATORS ARISING

ETCHED INTO MY MEMORY IS the first time I was exposed to cage fighting in the form of a television advertisement. The disturbing commercial featured a woman clinging to a fenced cage, pulling it back and forth in a frenzy, screaming wildly at the fighters within. Chosen by the producers for its obvious shock value, it was definitely effective. Even a couple of decades ago, I sensed something bigger was going on behind the advertised event, much more than just a new entertaining venue for an evening brawl.

What I eventually uncovered was a story of epic proportions—a story that spans thousands of years and took me back to the ancient Romans and their insatiable lust for blood sports. Through my research, the Roman Empire became more than just a distant, hazy entity, with little relevance to the realities of our everyday twenty-first century. It was a journey which uncovered a profound realization of just how connected our human nature is to the vestiges of our history. Rome's sophistication, civilization, yet humanness (minus the suits and ties) became more real to me than ever. With this renewed reality, I came to see how the influences of this distant civilization permeate our very own culture more than we might even dare to acknowledge.

Many of us growing up in the West are not fully cognizant of the dynamic impact which Christianity has had upon Western Civilization. This fact became glaringly apparent as I studied the ramifications which occurred when Christianity collided head-on with the mighty Roman Empire—reverberations which can be felt right down to our present day. Christ's blood on the cross and the blood and testimony of early, simple saints rocked the Roman Empire to its core. The church's love for people and their temporal and eternal well-being spoke against the brutalities of the day.

The early Christians and their humanness, formerly so distant, became very real to me. It brought back memories of reading *Augustine's Confessions* and the amazement I felt thinking that this man who lived about 1600 years ago could write in such a way that it seemed as if it was written only yesterday. My research was no longer just factual but actual as I became connected to the saints of old as part of the family of God. No longer were they just names in a history book.

This story is still relevant today as society grapples with how much damage will be tolerated in the ensuing "concussion crisis" and its own resurrection of blood sports. Though we will not find the return of gladiators mentioned in the pages of Scripture, we do discover that the Bible does point to a New Roman Empire that will emerge in the last days. Could it be that the bloodstained entertainment which was at the core of ancient Rome and the present global resurrection of this phenomenon are evidence that the new world that is emerging coincides with what Scripture tells us will occur?

The victory of the early Church with its influence upon the Roman Empire did not come without its problems as the power of Christianity was hijacked by those who sought to steer it in ways that were even contrary to the teachings of Christ. As Rome collapsed morally from within, the Church has had its own battle down through the ages to keep moral decay and doctrinal error out while maintaining love and unity within—a miracle only achieved through Christ.

As then, so now, there are those who seek to redefine Christianity in ways that are dangerous to the flock. One of the principal reasons I wrote this book was to bring to the forefront of the Christian consciousness the infiltration and popularity of cage fighting within the visible Church itself. Some may feel this whole topic has no relevance for us today, but I believe this book will show otherwise. Perhaps through understanding the history of blood sports and what the Bible teaches with respect to the rise of a "New Rome," a new generation of believers will come forth to mirror the early Church and not embrace the things of the world such as this. *Gladiators Arising: Blood-Bought vs. Blood Sport* is about life issues and eternal life issues. My desire in exposing these truths is to remind readers of the purity, power, message, and subsequent victory of the early Church. It is my hope that it will encourage us to evaluate our place in this epic story and how the Author of this story (the Lord Jesus) would have us respond.

CHAPTER 1

ENTER THE RING

LIGHTNING HAD ENDURED YET ANOTHER long, restless night. Wide awake and hours before daybreak, he lay in the silence of his bedroom, the adrenaline already pumping through him. Most of the night had been spent playing each of his former fights through his mind, reliving past glories as well as humiliating losses, and going over strategies for his upcoming bout. Only rarely had he tasted defeat; but as infrequent as they were, each one haunted him and cost him sleepless nights like this one.

His only fight during the past year had ended in yet another victory, but it had also resulted in his first serious injury. After months of rehabilitation and training, he had finally been cleared by the doctors. He was now ready to make his dramatic return. Today was to be the culmination of his life's ambition, the day he had been training for ever since he was a young boy. He would face the most challenging opponent of his career, but victory would mean he would finally rise to the very pinnacle of his profession.

When the first light of dawn finally appeared at his window, the familiar, demanding voice that had dogged his sleep for the past several years interrupted his reverie. Quickly, he jumped from bed, pulled his gear together, and gathered with the rest of the fight team. After a quick breakfast, they all began making their way through the city's crowded streets to the downtown stadium.

Once again, he was amazed to see his very own name on several of the billboards along their route, highlighting the fact that his bout was scheduled as the main event of the day. During the past several months, Lightning's personal popularity had soared to the extent that most of the shops near the stadium even carried his action figure. He laughed quietly to himself at the thought.

The core of the city was already alive and bustling with activity as they entered the downtown area. He knew that within hours, the nearby stadium would begin to be packed with thousands of fans. The music would be pumping, and the special effects would be doing their part in stirring up the multitudes even further, building the excitement to a fever pitch for the day's eventual climax—his bout.

Lightning could almost taste the tension as he and the others entered the stadium to enact their parts in the opening ceremonies. When the formalities finally ended, Lightning was given the opportunity to collect himself in the quiet of his dressing room. There, he could once again rehearse his strategies and focus his thoughts. In the welcoming solitude, Lightning managed to still his jangled nerves and channel his energy. Breathing deeply, he released himself once more into the focused calm he had trained himself so hard to achieve.

Finally, his moment came. An official entered his dressing room and beckoned. Slowly, he rose and walked the long, covered aisleway leading to the very heart of the stadium. At his appearance, the crowd erupted into a wild, exuberant frenzy. Lightning paused for a long moment and looked upward into the mass of his adoring followers, all gazing at him with an almost reverential awe. Finally, he raised his arms to acknowledge the cheers, then made his way over to where his opponent waited.

An official slipped between the two fighters and carefully reviewed the rules of engagement, but Lightning's mind was too focused to take in anything of what was being said. His eyes were locked on his opponent's, every muscle in his body poised and ready.

As the official stepped aside and signaled the beginning of the match, the two combatants cautiously began circling one another, then came together in a furious tangle of blows and counter-blows. Immediately, the crowd was on its feet, screaming its encouragement and egging each of the combatants on to even greater efforts. At times, the fight would subside and then reignite in a flurry of blows, which rained back and forth so rapidly, they were almost invisible to the human eye.

It was obvious to all that the two men were evenly matched, which only further ignited the passion of the crowd. Suddenly, from nowhere, a blow to Lightning's head knocked the fighter onto his back. Lightning, though, recovered quickly. Dazed, he managed to roll to his right and was back on his feet, now more determined than ever.

The desperation of the attack that followed caught Lightning's opponent completely off-guard, leaving him stunned and reeling. Lightning, pressing his advantage, feinted to the left, then lunged forward, ready to deliver the final, devastating blow. Almost immediately, however, he realized his miscalculation. His opponent's unorthodox counterattack appeared almost as if in slow motion; and the blow which knocked Lightning to the ground, he never even saw coming.

Attack! He knew he had to get back up and press his earlier advantage. His eyes darted desperately, trying to determine how he might reestablish his initiative, but he knew at the same time that it was over. Reluctantly, gritting his teeth, he signaled his submission to the official. Immediately, the referee jumped onto the ground between the combatants, and the fight was ended.

Lightning lay where he had fallen, looking helplessly up at his opponent, who loomed as a shadow over him, his fist clenched, his leering countenance pushed tauntingly to within inches of Lightning's own face. As Lightning attempted to lift his head, he could only feel the blade of his opponent's sword pressing against his neck.[1]

COULD WE BE LIKE THEM?

At first glance, one may envision this narrative taking place in a modern American city, until the introduction of the sword in the last sentence.

The story highlights the unexpected similarities between what is termed "modern gladiators" and the "ancient gladiators" of Rome. Garret Fagan, in his groundbreaking work titled *The Lure of the Arena*, offers a very different perspective to the unfounded confidence that we in the West are nothing like the ancients. He concludes his analysis by saying, "Appreciation of the psychological dynamics that coursed through those far-away spectators leads to the rather more unsettling realization that the lure of the brutalities staged in the Roman arena may well lie closer to home than many of us might think."[2]

How close are we to these brutalities staged in Rome? The truth is modern gladiators have arrived. The *Los Angeles Times* highlights its arising in the article titled, "The Life of a UFC Wife: The Modern Gladiators Do Battle, You Feel the Pain." The article relays how she can, or can't, handle her husband facing the carnage of a fight and states, "'But whether she can handle it or not, it can't stop it from happening,' Welcome to America's blood sport."[3]

Ultimate Fighting Championship is a "sport" that puts two combatants in an octagon-shaped cage to fight until one is either knocked out, unable to continue, or submits by what is termed "tapping out." Head strikes, choking, and pounding on a grounded opponent are just a few ways in which this can be accomplished. In the realm of Mixed Martial Arts (MMA), UFC is the equivalent of the National Football League or National Hockey League in their respective areas. It is also one of the fastest-growing sports in the world.[4]

Often, any opposition to the sport is sharply criticized, and one of the biggest complaints of modern Mixed Martial Arts fighters and fans is that many people do not understand the sport. Critics miss the finer details of the art, and those who are concerned about its brutality are just ignorant. But quotes like, "The first thing you notice is the blood, [sic] the floor looks like a slaughterhouse's,"[5] do not endear UFC to many opponents, no matter how the sport is dressed up. Whether we agree with it, oppose it, or sit on the fence, a walk-through history has many valuable lessons for us all.

GLADIATORS

Unlike many modern conceptions of gladiatorial contests as being a free-for-all (as Hollywood might portray), what emerges from the corridors of ancient history tell a different story. What kind of similarities can we find between ancient gladiators and those who are termed modern gladiators? They are actually quite striking. The UFC itself picked up on the connection. Their introductory video for many years included a gladiator suiting up for battle.

Roman gladiators were groomed in training centers. "A *ludus* [gladiatorial school] represents one of the most extreme examples of fighting club memberships in world history."[6] These centers were much like the fight clubs that are popping up all over North America as MMA is on its meteoric rise. Archaeological evidence shows that some of these gladiators were trained as children before they hit puberty.[7]

The gladiatorial teams, as today, travelled from city to city putting on shows for the masses at the local stadiums. These stadiums, as in large city centers of our day, were scattered throughout the Roman Empire. The greatest of these stadiums was the Colosseum in the capital city of Rome. This structure alone held between fifty thousand to eighty thousand fans, "becoming a model of design for arenas empire-wide."[8] Our modern word *arena* is from the Latin word *harena*, which means "sand." This sand was used to mop up the blood of the slain.

The Latin word *gladius* means "sword." The *Merriam-Webster Dictionary,* in its definition for *gladiator,* includes "a trained fighter; especially: a professional boxer."[9] This makes the meaning for the word *gladiator* broader than just its technical term. These events were not just afternoon brawls but were, as today, carefully choreographed shows. The Roman fighters made their entrance in a pre-fight exhibition, and the show was enlivened by special effects. As in our time, yet using different techniques, "Great care was taken to erect impressive staging in the form of artificial hills and landscapes, elaborate frameworks or trapdoors that suddenly yawned in the sand to discharge fresh animals or combatants."[10]

Music through the ages has been a powerful tool to arouse emotion; as rock music pounds today when combatants enter center stage of the cage, so music was a big part of the ancient arena.[11] These were well-planned and staged fights to please the masses of cheering crowds. Roman gladiators who performed well were crowd favorites; they could receive the prized wooden sword (rudis), while today's fighters look to gain and maintain the prized "belt."

BIG BUSINESS

Like the modern-day UFC posters that find their way onto the doors of bars and restaurants featuring the main event fighters, so advertisements for games were painted on walls.[12] As rankings and fighter profiles are important today, so were they to the gladiator and to his fans in ancient times. Inscriptions were written to allow fans to know who had won and who was allowed to see another day. The more popular a gladiator, the less likely he was to die in the ring.

The gladiators, though often slaves, became the stars of their time. Any MMA fan will be able to tell you who the stars of UFC are; and with it becoming mainstream, fighters are becoming household names. As today— when fighters take names such as "The Nightmare," "Rampage," and "The Serial Killer,"—so gladiators also had their own names such as "Stinger," "Blade," and "Pretty Boy." "That is to say, gladiators took stage names."[13]

There is no doubt that UFC adds a sexual element to its show. While flexing their muscles at their weigh-ins, UFC fighters are staged with scantily clad women. The Roman gladiators, too, were seen as sex symbols. One ancient source states, "Celadus the Thraex, the sigh of the girls."[14] When women gladiators fought (which is an emerging phenomenon in MMA), the sexual element was also a big draw. This was big business all around with promoters arranging the fights. As with UFC, gladiators had action figures that represented them.[15] Go online, or visit your local shopping mall, and you may be able to locate the latest UFC toy figurines.

One of the reasons the early form of UFC did not attract mainstream attention is that it was not professional. Matches were often uneven, fast, and brutal. UFC gained lasting popularity when weight divisions were created; they embraced regulations, and the fighting took on a "respectable edge." The Romans also didn't like the idea of an uneven match. They, like modern fans, enjoyed knowing the strengths, potential weaknesses, and style of a particular fighter. This knowledge intrigued the informed Roman spectator. Fagan states, "much more than raw bloodlust was at work, since appreciation of gladiatorial artistry was not in itself an indulgence of sadism."[16] After basic training, each fighter was trained in a particular fighting art (though sometimes the gladiators were trained in multiple disciplines).[17]

Today, UFC is almost synonymous with MMA. Mixed Martial Arts is the combining of many disciplines; yet each fighter will have his or her own strengths and potential weaknesses. Unlike boxing, MMA unites all forms of martial arts, which is one of the reasons it is challenging boxing as a global phenomenon.

The gladiatorial fight itself had rules that were enforced by umpires, not unlike modern-day referees. As in Mixed Martial Arts, a sign of submission was allowed to the endangered or defenseless combatant. MMA has what is called "tapping out," while Roman gladiators could lift their finger or hand. Once a Roman fighter had submitted, the referee would jump in to ensure a judgment was allowed. The crowds today can boo; but for the ancient gladiator, this show of displeasure meant death.

THE LOSER WINS

One particularly interesting similarity is that a fighter's ability to put on a show was as important as winning the fight. In UFC 129 in Toronto, Mark Hominick made his debut in the Ultimate Fighting Championship. He lost his fight, and yet he was the one who stole the show before fifty-five thousand fans.[18] It was Georges St. Pierre, the super star, who won his fight and yet was apologizing to his fans for his less-than-sterling performance. "In fact, to those who don't appreciate the finer points of MMA fighting, you could say it was a letdown. In fact, by the fourth round the fans were whistling their disappointment. By the fifth, some of them were booing."[19] Hominick won the hearts of the fans because despite having a tomato-sized lump on his head, he continued to fight aggressively and almost pulled out a victory.

The Romans loved the fearless fighter. "Arena spectators were knowledgeable and knew what a good fight looked like; they recognized deft moves and smart maneuvers; they could tell the difference between a humdrum fight-by-the-book and something special."[20] Respect was quickly lost when a fighter ran from his opponent; thus, if you showed weakness, you were despised. This is reminiscent of when Forest Griffin (former UFC Champion) was defeated and ran out of the arena. He did not win any points from fans. There is a certain expectation of "respect" and "respectability," as defined within the world of MMA. The same expectation held true for the Roman fans.

Surviving the fight was the first priority, yet many non-fatal injuries were also sustained by ancient fighters. Because the gladiators were such financial assets and some were well-paid themselves, they were prized and given the best medical treatment available.[21] Modern doctors are amazed at the level of competency their ancient counterparts had in looking after the injured.

Medical clearance is also important for UFC and MMA fighters. Now, in Ontario, results from a CT (computed tomography) scan is mandatory sixty days before every fight (for out-of-province fighters). As in ancient times, it is the up-and-comer whose life and limbs tend to be at greater risk. Yet even for the professionals, the dangers are great. In UFC 129, an American combatant was forbidden to fight because it was discovered that he had a brain hemorrhage, a very dangerous condition. In addition to this, though not threatening his attempt for combat, he had suffered a ruptured testicle as a result of a kick to the groin weeks earlier during training.[22]

THE PARADOX

So, what are we to make of the similarities between ancient and modern gladiatorial displays? Without yet delving into the factors of why we are not so distinct from the ancient West, some initial observations are important. Certainly applicable for today, Tertullian, an early church writer, wrote, "The same man who tries to break up or denounces a quarrel in the streets which has come to fisticuffs will in the stadium applaud fights far more dangerous."[23] Tertullian observed that a man may see a fight outside the arena and be angered by its lawlessness and yet, in the arena, cheer on a more brutal fight.

The strange paradox rings true in our society as well. After observing an MMA event, fans may feel compelled to call the police if a fight breaks out on the street. They may abhor the act because it is an illegal offense to fight in this public forum. The police would arrest and charge the offenders. If they choked, punched, or kicked each other, they would be quickly removed. Yet amazingly, these same illegal activities in the MMA octagon are applauded by the fans.

In his writing *On the Spectacles*, Tertullian observed another strange paradox in his day. "They love whom they punish, [sic] they devalue whom they admire; the art they glorify, [sic] the artist they stigmatize! . . . Their authors, at the height of their popularity, are in disgrace."[24] Could this same paradox be seen today?

In MMA, there is much talk about respect. Yet, the question remains: What is respect? Is it respectful to punch someone in the face, choke them, and enter a ring for the purpose of subjecting them to concussions (i.e. brain damage)? Yes, these men and women are admired; but in reality, they are devalued. They are loved when they brutalize or are brutalized. MMA as an art form is lifted up, while the artist is left broken on the mat.

There is no doubt that differences presently exist between then and now. Many gladiators were slaves or captives, the lowest of the low in Roman society, and were called *infamia* along with actors and prostitutes. Yet we find the lure of the games was so great that many free individuals would also find themselves volunteering to enter the ranks of these fighters.[25]

They also wore various amounts of armor and used different types of weapons to fight their opponents. Though they would fight to the death, one study of the early Empire found that about ninety percent of trained gladiators lived to see another day.[26] The debate continues as to how many actually died in a given competition. All that is to say, as we have seen, that there was much more going on than just two men fighting to the death.

These present differences need not comfort us too much. Perceptive historians are intrigued by the questions: Could we be like them? Is the lure of the brutalities staged in the Roman arena closer to home than many of us might think? It is a good reminder to all that the ancient Roman Empire imploded by moral decline from within, and any attempt to retrace its steps, wittingly or unwittingly, will only bring the same result.

Professor Andrew Wallace says, "Could we be like it or are they completely different from us? Are they monsters, did they work differently as human beings?—and I think we know that there is a bit in us that is absolutely there with the Romans. We could be like them."[27]

CHAPTER 2

THE VICTORY OF THE CROSS

THE FIRST LIGHT OF DAWN had barely peered through his bedroom window when Claudius was jolted from his bed. The news that his sister brought that morning was devastating. It was bad enough that Justus, their long-time friend, had been arrested, but his sister's news would get even worse.

His sister told him that it had all started innocently enough when Justus went to visit some new acquaintances on a business matter. His wife, Maria, reported that shortly after this meeting, several Roman soldiers abruptly arrived at their home and dragged Justus off to prison. Claudius knew Justus to be a most personable man, who never missed an opportunity to share his faith in Christ; but in a society governed by the Romans, Claudius also knew this brought great risks. Strong and hardworking, Justus was a man firm in his convictions, who sought to love his enemies, even those who mocked him.

It now seemed obvious that someone had taken offense at Justus' newfound faith and reported him to the authorities. Claudius' sister told him that those who attended the house fellowship in Justus' home were now gathering there to pray for his release. Word was out that Justus refused to recant his faith. He was given time to comply or face entering the stadium to die.

The official charge—his refusal to offer incense to the emperor and worship the Roman gods. Claudius knew that it would have been a simple matter for Justus to bow to their demands and gain his release, but he would confess that only Jesus Christ was Lord and would not worship the emperor's image.

Claudius quickly hugged his weeping sister, then dashed out into the street. He knew he had to get to Justus' home on the other side of the city to support Maria and her children and encourage the small house fellowship meeting there.

Claudius was winded by the time he passed the arena in the downtown area of the city. As he looked up at the dreadful stadium, he began trembling with anger, the tears welling up in his eyes.

Many Christians had died for their faith—believers who had left behind amazing stories of courage and perseverance. Claudius was thankful that the testimonies of these martyrs had done much to embolden their brothers and sisters in the faith, but the pain was almost overwhelming. A loud, gruff voice ordering Claudius to move out of the way jarred him back to the present reality.

When he arrived at Justus' house, he was greeted by a weeping Maria. Her three small children clung desperately to her garments. Several other brothers and sisters in the faith were already gathered together in prayer, crying out to the Lord. Tears once again welled in Claudius' eyes as he took in the scene before him. *How long can this go on? How long, O Lord, must we suffer in this way?*

Claudius knew he could not fight to bring Justus back to his family. His only means of fighting could be the battle he would wage on his knees. It seemed that only he and this tiny band of Christians stood alone against the might of the Roman army, clinging desperately to a hope that one day the impossible would happen and that Christ would be recognized as Lord of all.[28]

THE CROSS TRIUMPHS

There stands today in the midst of the Roman Colosseum a cross. The cross, in fact, was placed at the very location where the emperors sat in all their pomp and glory. The same site where they, along with the cheering crowds, indulged themselves in a barbaric spectacle of unimagined cruelty.

The impossible had indeed happened. The erecting of the cross in this once-glorious stadium now stands as an ironic paradox. Christ and His small band of persecuted followers had overcome the might of the Roman Empire, their sacrificial influence sweeping across the entire world. The One sarcastically called the "King of the Jews" by the Romans is now remembered in this symbolic way in the very heart of Rome, triumphant over emperors and even an empire.

The ancient emperors of Rome are obscure to many people today, yet globally remembered is a humble Builder (Greek-Tekton), Who was crucified under Pontius Pilate, a Roman governor in a remote part of the Empire.

The cross is an apt picture of the influence of biblical Christianity, which spread not by the sword, but through love and suffering. As the official Western Roman Empire fell, the true congregation of believers continued to rise. The ruins of the broken Colosseum stand as a reminder of the kingdom of man and its ultimate end versus the enduring Kingdom of God.

How did a seemingly haphazard and persecuted little group influence the Roman Empire by which the whole of Western civilization and beyond would profit? Where did its power lie? "The practical application of charity [love] was probably the most potent single cause of Christian success . . . Christian charity expressed itself in care for the poor, for widows and orphans, in visits to brethren in prison or condemned to the living death of labor in the mines, and in social action in time of calamity like famine, earthquake, pestilence or war."[29] It was a passionate commitment of love for their Savior, love for people, and deep concern for their temporal and eternal well-being that drove the little congregation (today known as the early Church) forward.

THE ADVANCEMENT

So monumental was the influence of Jesus Christ, that an eruption of magnificent proportions exploded across the Roman world. In its humble beginnings, a small group of believing Jews started a movement that continues to advance down to this very day.

These Jewish believers did not feel that they were traitors to Israel or deniers of the Law of Moses, but recognized the Promised One of old, Who "bore the sin of many" (Isa. 53:12) and would "sprinkle many nations" (Isa. 52:15).

This One was a descendant of their father Abraham and would be the One through Whom "all the families of the earth will be blessed" (Gen. 12:3). Jesus, called the Christ, was the One Whose death was prophesied in the Old Testament; it was to take place before the destruction of the Jewish Temple (Dan. 9:25-26) which, unbeknownst to them, would happen in A.D. 70 under a Roman warrior named Titus. This Titus later bore the name Emperor and completed the building of the once-glorious Roman Colosseum.

In A.D. 64, a great fire swept through Rome; and Emperor Nero, having fallen out of favor with many, blamed it on the Christians. By that time, Christianity had made such amazing inroads into Roman society that, prior to the fire, the apostle Paul could pass on greetings from "Caesar's household" to the Philippian church (Phil. 4:22). Over time, the threat of Christianity within Rome grew. Nero's actions set "a precedent that magistrates had condemned Christians put to death because they were Christians and on no other charge."[30] Though true, its practice varied, since the persecution of Christians ebbed and flowed in severity and location, culminating at the Great Persecution.

Emperor Domitian proclaimed himself to be "Master and God." A test of loyalty to him as ruler was instituted, and "the customary oath 'by the genius of the emperor' became officially obligatory."[31] As with all the Emperors, to varying degrees, Christians were in threat because they were seen as "atheists" (believing in only One true God). Rejecting the empire's gods put them at odds with Roman law and the demands of rulers. Performing various rituals and a denial of Christ set the offender free. But the unbending loyalty of these believers was a threat to a "tolerant society," which was intolerant only of those who held to one absolute truth, an increasing trend we see today.

Though generally recognized as honorable people and morally upright, this did not protect them from the arena. Tertullian himself would exclaim that if something catastrophic happened in the empire, the cry was at once, "the Christians to the lions [sic]."[32] Christians, like other criminals, suffered a wide variety of different forms of execution.

The early Christians did not see themselves as a sect of Judaism, but ministers of the Good News to fellow sinners. They came proclaiming that the Jewish Messiah, the Savior of the world, had come. This Good News was extended to the Gentiles (non-Jews) as well. Salvation was a gift of God and could not be earned by good works or a combination thereof: for "by grace you have been saved" (Eph. 2:5). Eternal life was given to those who, by God's grace, had repented and believed in the death, burial, and resurrection of the Lord Jesus.

Entrance into the Kingdom of God was evidenced by doing the will of the Father. Obedience, good works, and love were fruits of a person who had the risen Lord dwelling within them. Only through God's power could one love their enemies and pray for those who persecuted them (Matt. 5:44).

The Old Testament was foundational to the Jewish and Gentile Church. It was the bedrock of the New Testament. As the Church exploded west toward Rome, it took with it the core values rooted in Jewish thought. These truths clashed for centuries against pagan idolatry and lust for bloody spectacles. "For the Jews, culture was indissolubly bound up with piety and morality . . . References to gladiators in Hebrew texts are virtually non-existent."[33]

Its absence is not all that surprising when we understand why. It was an abhorrence to Jews to see men killed for the pleasure of the crowd. "For Jews it meant an open challenge to the customs they held in high honor."[34] Their moral basis was the Old Testament, and the central truth was that every individual was created in the image of God.

FIRST PRINCIPLES

The book titled *The Beginning of Wisdom* by Dr. Kass brings out the point that "Genesis is punctuated with human attempts to be radically self-sufficient"[35] (i.e., without God). The Bible is full of examples of people who wanted to do life on their own terms—to "be like God" (Gen. 3:5).

With the book of Genesis as a backdrop, Dr. Kass sees dangers in the "unbounded ambitions of modern democratic man."[36] What are the limits to cloning? What are the limits to abortion, infanticide, and euthanasia? What we see is the age-old dilemma. Are humans going to make the decisions of life, or is God? In the end, our worldview will determine how we define what a human being is and how we live.

The New York Times author Edward Rothstein wrote a review on Dr. Kass' work titled, "A Bioethicist's Take on Genesis." He poses a series of relevant questions: "But what compels an avowed secularist to adopt Mr. Kass's views of 'dignity'? Without a belief in God, what are the first principles by which human behavior can be limited? What contemporary covenant could possibly help resolve such issues?"[37]

For ancient believers, the answer lay embedded in Genesis 1:27: "God created man in His own image, in the image of God He created him; male and female He created them." This verse was the bedrock first principle for human dignity.

Modern scholars have various theories as to why individuals from various walks of life were concerned about such displays. After a number of suggestions, classicist Dr. Thomas Wiedemann concludes, "Finally—and perhaps most crucially—there need have been little or no connection between the hostility against the games, whether by philosophers, Church fathers, or even emperors, and their decline."[38] Wiedemann would have us believe that no connection exists between these individuals, their sense of morality, and the decline of the Roman games. This conclusion is surely wrong.

This understanding is similar to that of individuals who would like to see no connection or danger in our return to gladiators, for "we are surely not like them." Scholars may, at times, divide humanity into their own disconnected spheres. Yet, not only is humanity biologically connected today by a very real ancestral Adam and ancestral Eve as one human race, but everyone also has an innate knowledge of right and wrong.

In our human "hardware," we all know murder is wrong, especially if the gun is pointed at us or our children. Whether Greek philosopher, Jewish,

Christian, or avowed atheist, we all have a sense of morality. The imparted "software" can vary greatly, but the "hardware" remains. There are many non-Christians today who would see and sense that there is something terribly wrong with Ultimate Fighting.

The question again arises: What source do we have for authoritative first principles? On what basis can we ultimately judge whether gladiators and one of its most modern counterparts, UFC, are lawless and wrong? Yet, to properly understand the demise of the ancient gladiatorial games (though a very complex issue), it needs to be recognized that the enduring influence of Christianity and the lasting first principles of Genesis were its most powerful opponent.[1]

WHEN KINGDOMS COLLIDE

Gladiatorial fights first started being exhibited at funerals. They were "from ancient Etruscan funeral processions that made sacrifices to the gods of the underworld in honor of the deceased."[39] Slaves were made to fight to the death before the attendees. This practice was later used by the Romans, who put on gladiatorial fights dating from 264 B.C. and fading away after A.D. 401 (approximately seven hundred years).

At first it was for funerals, but the power of these spectacles to please crowds was quickly recognized as being economically and politically advantageous. Not only were these displays financially profitable, but in time, they became a significant display of power by local statesmen and those seeking office. Eventually, the emperors themselves used gladiatorial fights to show their power in order to win the loyalty of the people.

---

1   There is no doubt, as scholars often point out, that the "barbarians" who became a part of the Roman Empire and eventually took over leadership in Rome had a part in the dissolution of gladiatorial games. The conventional date for the fall of Rome is A.D. 476, when the capital fell to the Germanic hordes. These "barbarians" were often seen by Romans as safer and more moral than themselves. These "new" people saw no need for the games, and thus, they continued to fade away. But I think it needs to be added that this was not done in a vacuum. Christianity was already having influence outside the Roman Empire, and eventually, Christianity's influence would sweep over all of Europe. This is why I state that Christianity and its first principles were the most enduring opponent (both before the "hordes" and after) to the gladiatorial games.

The mammoth Colosseum took center stage in Rome, being one of about 230 amphitheaters throughout the area of the Roman Empire. It was a place where the masses were able to come for free and even see the emperor himself. The emperors used these displays to show everyone who actually held the power of life and death. This was a type of deterrent to crime, but also an opiate for the masses. Professor Kathleen Coleman comments, "I think it's important to realize how seductive the amphitheater was. All of the pomp and ceremony, the extravagance of it all must have been addictive."[40] A feeling of unity was suddenly created when people came together with the same interests and could have their emotions aroused in a "safe" environment.

Augustine, an early church leader, chronicled the power and lure of the arena in the story highlighting one of his friends, Alypius. He was an individual who seemingly had strong moral values and had to be dragged into the arena by his friends. Alypius was convinced he was strong enough to resist and had every intention of keeping his eyes off the spectacle. But due to the lure of the boisterous crowd, he found himself staring with eyes wide open:

> The minute he saw blood, he was sipping animality, and turned no more away. With eyes glued to the spectacle, he absentmindedly gulped down frenzies. He took a complicit joy in the fighting, and was drunk with delight at the cruelty. No longer the person he was when he entered, he was now entered into the crowd, at one with those who forced him there. More—he stared, he shouted, he burned, he took away the madness he had found there and followed it back again, not only with those who had first drawn him, but dragging them and others on his own.[41]

As with anything addictive, the addiction not only calls one back again, but it comes beckoning with greater expectations. The games almost took on a life of their own because from emperor to emperor, the pressure to satisfy the expectations and cravings of the people grew. As we observe in Hollywood, the displays of violence that gripped viewers forty years ago are laughable to the audience today. Hollywood must produce more and more graphic material, so as to satisfy the expectations of those addicted to modern mass media. What we find is that people today and those in ancient times are not that different at all.

Fagan presses the question further, as he considers what the major draw was for people to the Roman amphitheater. He concludes that one of the primary lures of the arena was its ability to elicit powerful sensations through group dynamics. This social identity and power enabled fans to help shape the course of events. "At the arena, they were lords for a day and enjoyed a god-like power of life and death over others."[42]

This is a stunning comment because it really cuts to the heart of the issue. Here again is where the kingdom of man and the Kingdom of God collide. When mankind's reason becomes the basis for law and order, he becomes the arbiter of his own domain. Humans continually seek to take the place of God.

Whether it is a fan in the seat or a leader of a nation, the desire to enjoy god-like power is a tremendous lure. To enter uninhibited into the arena and cast aside that which is normally "forbidden" has enormous appeal. From Emperor Domitian declaring himself to be "Lord and God," to Hitler becoming a god to the Germans, the kingdom of man has always attempted to replace and then be "as God."

OPPOSITION

With a unified voice, the early Church took its stand against gladiators and other immoral attractions of the Roman Empire. As those seeking to speak for the Kingdom of God, they envisioned the Roman arena as a place where— as Fagan rightly points out—no one involved was in a neutral position. The crowds were emotionally, psychologically, and even physically involved with their gyrating.

In our modern Western society, it is easy to see individuals as just that: "individuals." But the reality is, we are part of a whole. This is why culture, communities, and sub-cultures have tremendous effects on the way people view life and live. Our connection with each other allows us to live vicariously through others. The definition of vicarious is that which is "experienced or realized through imaginative or sympathetic participation in the experience of another—'a vicarious thrill.'"[43] It need not always be a thrill. This is why a horror movie, though a non-reality, can evoke such terror in the audience.

The early church writer Theophilus of Antioch wrote, "We are forbidden so much as to witness shows of gladiators, lest we become partakers and abettors of murders."[44] This is actually a very insightful comment. First, through this vicarious participation, there was actually a guilt and pollution involving murder upon the cheering crowd. Secondly, it shows that one community had formally forbidden participation in the activities of another. So seriously did the leadership take the issue that trainers of gladiators were excluded from the Church.

Wiedemann surprisingly asserts, "Nor is it clear that it was the objections of those who were implacably opposed to gladiatorial displays (as many Christian writers were, though as we shall see not for 'humanitarian' reasons) that led to imperial legislation against them."[45] The early Church would be aghast at the suggestion that there was no humanitarian reason behind their Christian opposition of gladiatorial displays.

This claim is totally objectionable in light of the facts. Of course, they were concerned about people. If a church leader spoke against the idolatry of the games, the pollution of the games, or its lawlessness, it was for the betterment of those created in God's image. Certainly, the demise of the games was complex, but to obscure any direct link between Christianity and the games' demise is, again, surely wrong.

Irenaeus, a church leader in Lyons, condemned those that "do not even keep away from that blood spectacle hateful both to God and men, in which gladiators either fight with wild beasts, or singly encounter one another."[46] Here is again an appeal to the first principles that it was hateful to God. Why? Because those who were created in God's image were being exploited and bloodied for the enjoyment of the crowd.

Not only this, but it was blood money. Tatian, an Assyrian and early writer, exclaimed, "He who is chief among you collects a legion of blood-stained murderers, engaging to maintain them . . . The robber commits murder for the sake of plunder, but the rich man purchases gladiators for the sake of their being killed."[47]

When lawlessness increases, then also do injustices. Tertullian, an early church apologist from Carthage, declared, "Certain it is that innocent men are sold as gladiators to serve as victims of public pleasure. Even in the case of those who are condemned to the games, what a preposterous idea is it that, in atonement for a smaller offense, they should be driven to the extreme of murder."[48]

The first principles of Genesis undergirded the early Church's disdain for the spectacles. They were not against justice, but injustice. The displays of gladiatorial shows for public pleasure and the injustices of the spectacle were hateful both to Jews and Christians alike. For to murder a man created in the image of God was tantamount to attacking God Himself.

Yet the irony was, as Tertullian put it, "The blood of the martyrs is the seed of the Church."[49] It was actually the murder of Christians before cheering crowds and their ability to love their enemies that had a profound effect on the dissolution of gladiators and the transformation of the Roman Empire. The last recorded gladiatorial fight in the city of Rome was fought in A.D. 404.

GLADIATORIAL DEATH BLOW

The following account is found in *The Ecclesiastical History* of Theodoret:

> Honorius, who inherited the empire of Europe, put a stop to the gladiatorial combats which had long been held at Rome . . . A certain man of the name of Telemachus had embraced the ascetic life. He had set out from the East and for this reason had repaired to Rome. There, when the abominable spectacle was being exhibited, he went himself into the stadium, and, stepping down into the arena, endeavored to stop the men who were wielding their weapons against one another.

The spectators of the slaughter were indignant . . . [and] stoned the peacemaker to death. When the admirable emperor was informed of this he . . . put an end to that impious spectacle.[50]

Later, Theoderic the Great (c. A.D. 500) would himself put an end to the mutilating "sport" of boxing for the oft-stated reason: it was an insult to God because it disfigures the face, the image of God.[51] [2]

CHRISTIAN OR CHRISTIANIZED?

There has been much debate as to the official reasons for the fall of Rome, and volumes have been written to analyze what actually happened. Without getting into the controversy, it is safe to say that, unofficially, Rome underwent a massive transformation. One can even question if its legacy has ever completely fallen. The topic is beyond the scope of this book, but it is important to ask, "What was the impact of Christianity on the Roman world in which it found itself?" To best understand what took place, we need to understand the internal essence of Christianity.

Christianity is not a nation with borders and political leaders; it is a global family. This family is without borders, social class, or ethnic barriers; and its love can reach into unexpected spheres. Though the Christians were persecuted for about 250 years, an amazing turn of events happened in Rome in the early fourth century. The Emperor Galarius tried to crush the church during The Great Persecution initiated in A.D. 303. Finally, "the vicious emperor gave up the fight against Christianity, issuing the Edict of Toleration."[52]

In A.D. 311, Christianity's influence pushed forward from being merely tolerated to becoming, within that century, the official state religion (A.D. 381). This change of events created many benefits but also came with its own problems. The power and influence of the Church was now recognized, and there is no doubt that many leaders took full advantage of the turning tide.

---

2   The image of God would properly be defined by many as a spiritual reality, rather than a physical one. Yet, despite a different definition used above, the importance of the image of God is highlighted.

It is at this point that scholars begin to recognize the inconsistencies that started to arise. They see that "Christian" leaders were doing things that were not very Christian. Wiedemann takes up this issue at length by pointing out the paradox in regards to gladiators. In A.D. 325, Constantine issued a rescript stating, "We therefore utterly forbid the existence of gladiators." Yet it is recorded, "Three years after the Berytus ruling, a gladiatorial contest took place in Antioch, a city which had a reputation of being exceptionally 'Christian.'"[53]

How could this be? How do we have a "Christian Rome" with such hypocrisy? Other scholars can be cited as stating that "Christian" leaders in Rome actually supported the gladiatorial games; "they just stop killing fellow Christians."[54]

What do we make of all of this inconsistency? The key to understanding this is within the teachings of Christ: "Why do you call Me, 'Lord, Lord,' and do not do what I say?" (Luke 6:46). Many would claim to be followers of Christ, and yet their actions showed the contrary. This lack of substance and commitment explains why it took nearly a century for the death blow to be dealt to gladiatorial fights in Rome. Many instances can be cited where individuals look back in history and see atrocities allowed or carried out by "Christians," and yet there is nothing Christian about the atrocities. It is fair to ask: Was Rome now Christian or was it Christianized?

The simplicity of the Christian message is often lost when it is hijacked or takes on a purely institutionalized form. Even today, when many people think of the Church, they may only think of a building. Yet, the Bible never mentions the Church as a building, but as a family.

When Christianity became the state religion, the mixture of church and state further complicated matters. After a number of centuries, the Holy Roman Empire (800-1806) emerged and continued to fail at maintaining the familial structure of the true Church. Rome became an important center within the Holy Roman Empire, with the Pope effectually replacing the emperor in status and power in many ways. The Pope was not only a religious figure but an extremely powerful political figure.

When we look back in history, are we going to use the term Christian to mean anyone who claimed to be a Christian or those who acted in accordance with the life and teaching of the Lord Jesus? Like those who claimed Christianity and supported the gladiatorial spectacles, are we merely going to take them at their word or by word and deed? This answers the ironic question as to why the official church started to persecute and put to death those who sought to follow the Bible's truths. The hostility of those who had the outward appearance of being followers of Christ would actually be unleashed against true believers.

John Wycliffe (c. 1330-1384) was persecuted for translating the Bible into English and questioning the teaching and abuses of the official church. John Hus (c. 1369-1415) was burned at the stake for questioning many teachings not found in the Bible. William Tyndale (c. 1494-1536) was burned at the stake for translating the Bible into English from the original Hebrew and Greek. It was actually illegal to put the words of Jesus Christ into the language of the common people.

These abuses didn't happen only under the Roman Catholic Church, but also under the Church of England. One stunningly finds John Bunyan (c. 1628-1688) writing his famed *Pilgrim's Progress* from prison. Why? For preaching the Gospel of Christ. These individuals dared to question the institutionalized and politicized structures of their day and found themselves in serious trouble.

To be sure, the Messiah, Whom true believers follow, never caved to political pressure and never turned a blind eye to evil. He was brutalized and hung on a Roman cross. His enduring legacy was built upon truth and love, not compromise. The cross stands today in the Colosseum of Rome as a testimony of the enduring first principles, the lasting effects of love, and the influence of biblical Christianity.

Western civilization can never be understood if we neglect to understand the influence of Christianity upon it for centuries. Yet, the dawning of a marginalized Christian West, in which the Church is finding itself today, is revealing some rather uncomfortable questions: *Are we, as humans, fundamentally different from the Romans? Is there compromise in the Church in relation to the neo-gladiators of our day? Is the West on its way back to Rome?*

CHAPTER 3

THE NEW GLADIATORS

ICE STRAIGHTENED HIS TIE AS he looked intently into the full-length mirror in front of him. He breathed in deeply and pursed his lips together as he tugged at his suit jacket one last time. He then turned and walked slowly through his dressing room to the door where his team was waiting. Without a word, his coach and team quickly filed in behind Ice, then slowly followed him down the hallway to the press conference room.

As soon as he appeared, the media quickly swarmed around him, asking questions and requesting interviews. Most of their questions, however, were drowned out by the blaring music pouring out of a half dozen large speakers scattered around the room. Ice said nothing—his face an expressionless mask as the glaring lights of the television cameras were switched on. He could now barely make out anyone in the multitude of photographers scurrying about him and his entourage—walking backwards, crouching, all looking for the perfect shot.

Camera shutters rattled on, and flashes continued to burst around him as he walked steadily through the crowd, seemingly unfazed by the ruckus that enveloped him. "Chill," Ice said over his shoulder to his agitated teammates as he adjusted the title belt hanging over his shoulder. "They're just doing their job."

He paused for a moment at the bottom of a set of stairs leading up to the stage at the front of the room. Slowly and methodically, he mounted each step, almost as if he was calculating his every move until he finally reached the platform. There, across from him, stood his opponent, his dark eyes riveted on Ice's every move. With a deliberate swagger, Ice walked across the stage until he was only inches from the other man. He came to a stop and, for a long moment, stood facing his adversary, undaunted by his trash talk, toe-to-toe, nose-to-nose as the electricity of the moment crackled throughout the crowded room.

Suddenly, his opponent did a slight head fake, then lunged toward Ice, shoving him backward. The explosion that ensued quickly erupted into a pushing and shoving match. Caught off-guard, the announcer grabbed Ice, struggling with all his might to separate him from the other man. Finally, the members of each team were able to squeeze into the melee and drag the two opponents to separate areas of the platform.

Quickly, Ice shook himself free of his handlers and then turned toward his foe and pointed one finger in the other man's direction. At that moment, a hush fell among the assembled journalists and photographers so that Ice's next words seemed to echo throughout the room. "Deeds, not words," he said simply.

The room erupted in bedlam as Ice made his way back across the stage and down the stairs. In the background, above the noise, the voice of the announcer could be heard as he yelled into the microphone, "Save it for the cage, gentlemen. Save it for the cage."

HISTORY REPEATS?

> *"The Colosseum is now disused, but it has been replaced by the Octagon."*
> —Jad Seaman, Senior Analyst[55]

The Colosseum, once an architectural masterpiece, stands weathered and worn by the sands of time. Yet the emergence of a new, but similar venue for combat has arrived, known as the Octagon. The ramifications of such parallels are easily missed, but the question needs to be posed, "Are we on the road back to Rome?" Many may flatly deny this possibility, but the sense of comfort we all may experience—that surely, we could never go as far as the Romans—may truly be misplaced. Their brutality goes against all sensibilities. Yet Professor

Andrew Wallace of the British School of Rome states, "We ask all the time, could we be like these guys? Could we sit around, 50,000 people, in a great building watching someone die? Cheering."[56]

Often when we think of the Romans in terms of their love for blood sports, we see them as barbaric. Yet we need to realize they were the "civilized" of the ancient world. The barbarians were the ones who were outside the Empire. Rome had a highly sophisticated political system, centralized power, and cities throughout its domain. The desire for internal peace was summed up in what is called the "Pax Romana," the "Roman Peace." This was achieved through their domineering military strength and prowess. They even had surprising medical advancements.

Yet one of the areas in which the Romans felt a great sense of superiority was in technological achievements, such as roads, aqueducts, and buildings. One such example was the Roman Colosseum itself. "The Flavian Amphitheater (or *Amphiteatrum Flavium* as it was known to the Romans) opened for business in 80 CE in the reign of Titus . . . The finished building was like nothing seen before and situated between the wide valley joining the Esquiline, Palatine and Caelian hills, it dominated the city."[57]

They, like Westerners today, would be shocked to be called barbaric. Western civilization can boast of being those of the developed world versus those of the underdeveloped or developing societies. Technological and medical advances in the West are increasing at breakneck speed. Yet the very nature of mankind, when unchecked, has not changed. The heart of the matter is that as Christianity is increasingly marginalized and the belief that people are not created in God's image grows, the results begin to mirror that of ancient Rome.

THE MORAL DESCENT OF THE WEST

"There is a way which seems right to a man, But its end is the way of death."
—Proverbs 16:25

The shocking revelations of our present day should cause us, again, to question whether we falsely comfort ourselves. The *Washington Post* reports,

"One would assume that Nazi-like harvesting of human body parts for scientific experiments right here in the USA would be a major news story. Yet the American mainstream media has largely ignored it. Toss in the fact that the organization selling baby parts gets more than one-half billion dollars from the U.S. government and the story should be explosive. Why isn't it?"[58]

The harvesting and selling of baby body parts is not even an issue that grips the whole nation. What is happening? An *Evolution News and Views* article gives us a hint: "New Poll Reveals Evolution's Corrosive Impact on Beliefs about Human Uniqueness."[59] The high view of humans being created in the image of God has now been replaced by a new religious ideal. The article rightly highlights the profound impact that Darwinian evolutionism has had in our world.

We should awaken to the fact that within a span of fifty-plus years, during which Darwinian evolutionism has taken over the educational systems of the West, we are seeing the emergence and results of an increasingly godless society. Darwin's view of humanity cannot be kept neatly tucked away in the textbooks.

Prominent evolutionist Stephen Jay Gould wrote, "Biological arguments for racism may have been common before 1859, but they increased by orders of magnitude following the acceptance of evolutionary theory."[60] It should not surprise us that the eruption of racism, abortion, and euthanasia has also coincided with such a shift in worldview. It is a worldview that impacts the whole of society and now the world. Sixty years ago, the average person would not have conceived of the sale of baby body parts by a government-supported organization as ever happening within the United States of America, but it has been found to be a reality.

In a similar fashion to those sixty years ago, most people today would still be shocked and disgusted by the reality of the things that occurred within the arena. It seems so distant because we still can have a sense that it could not happen again. But the question is: Will history repeat itself?

The present-day media, though silent on some things, is well aware of others. "History repeats: After being among 55,000 people, cheering the fighters and asking for more action, it reminded me of the analogy: UFC fighters are the Roman Gladiators of our times. That night, the Rogers Center became the Roman Colosseum, coincidentally with almost the same amount of spectators. History, like economy, repeats."[61]

When we start examining how the media portrays the modern-day cage fights, there is little doubt that the link between the MMA fighter and Roman gladiator is well established. For many, the MMA fighter is the new gladiator, and the Arena and Octagon the new Colosseum. This is further evidence that we are surely on our way back to Rome's most violent and deadly entertainment. How far we have descended, perhaps only time will tell; but if we view history from the Greco-Roman Empire to our day as an arc, the descent is underway.

We can see early Christianity as injecting a whole new worldview into the Roman Empire. Its legacy is with us to this day. It was instrumental in bringing the Empire out of the depravity of the Colosseum. "It was the Christian gospel that finally put an end to the horrid games in the amphitheaters."[62] The message that humans were created in God's image and the recipients of God's love through Christ's sacrifice would impact the world. "With the rise of Christianity and the concurrent decline of the Roman Empire, pugilism as entertainment apparently ceased to exist for many centuries."[63] There may have been traces surfacing at different times and locations. "Traces of Pankration could be found in some parts of Greece and Turkey until its revival this past century."[64]

But we can now see the reversal of the arc rapidly descending upon our time. There are indications that we are farther along on the descent than many may think. The Christian worldview is under enormous attack, and the Darwinian worldview is globally entrenched and advancing. Its advance is not only in what people believe, but also in how they act.

If we look at the whole history of this blood sport, we must understand that it started back in the Greek world. Its original name was called Pankration.

Pankration means "all powers" or "all-encompassing." The goal was to master every aspect of the fight. In Greece, individuals would fight even to the death, in hand-to-hand combat. The rules were few—no biting and no eye gouging. The most well-known stage for this event became the Olympics. Individuals competed as representatives for their city-state. The olive wreath was the prized possession of the winner.

In the article *Roman Gladiator Games: The Origins of MMA*, it states: "Ancient Greek Pankration was the first historical instance of combined multi-art hand-to-hand fighting system. As such, current MMA may justifiably be termed an evolved form of Pankration that the Greeks of antiquity practiced."[65]

Greece, as with all great earthly powers, would decline; and Rome, with its overwhelming dominance, would then emerge onto the world stage. Yet, Rome was flexible enough to incorporate and accept ideas from other cultures. The Greco-Roman Empire easily accepted a form of the Greek's Pankration into its gladiatorial events. In making its way to Rome, it continued its evolution. Eventually, even weapons such as studded gloves were used in the fights. As Christianity's influence impacted Rome, in the year A.D. 393, the Roman Emperor Theodosius I banned the Olympic games as a Pagan Festival.[66] Pankration and boxing as part of the Olympics were also outlawed.

Later, boxing itself was specifically banned by another emperor. "Theodoric the Great argued that since the sport often led to death and severely disfigured the faces of its competitors, it was an abomination to God, because the Bible states that mankind is created in His image."[67] It was not until April 6, 1896, that the first modern Olympic Games were held again in Athens. No form of Pankration was included. Yet Pankration made a formal application to be included in the 2004 Olympic Games in Athens, but was denied.[68]

In light of these striking revelations, it would be overly simplistic if it were portrayed that between Rome and our current society, there were no displays of brutality. Historically, there have been public displays of torture and death, even in front of large crowds, often in the form of capital punishment and even by religious leaders. People's bloodlust did not disappear. Animals have been used in such displays as bull, dog, and cockfighting. In the realm of sport, jousting and other competitions could be brutal events. Dueling, though often outlawed, was a potentially deadly way to settle a dispute. Another form of fighting to settle disputes was called gouging. It was popular in the frontiers of the United States and was outlawed for its brutality.

But it is telling that Pankration (and its link to gladiators) is making its return this past century. Though practiced before in isolation, it has now exploded onto the world scene. UFC, MMA's highest level, has become one of the fastest growing sports in the world. There are millions of viewers worldwide. Its acceptance is going global, with only some resistance. It had been in its own fight for survival. But it appears to be here to stay.

UFC ALMOST TKO-ED

There comes a point on an arc where things almost become a freefall downward. The resistance is all but taken away, and the drop into the abyss has little to hold it back. In ancient biblical terms, "If the foundations are destroyed, what can the righteous do?" (Psalm 11:3). There does come a time where the current state within a society is in such decay, that a moral collapse becomes inevitable. It reaches critical mass. There is no doubt that God has pulled nations out of such moral decline—Israel being the great example. But this lies within the purposes and sovereignty of God.

Yet on an arc, some resistance can be detected. Such resistance can be illustrated toward the UFC itself. Its beginnings were in November, 1993, and it was to be a no-holds-barred slugfest. UFC was advertised with the same blunt force that would be introduced into the ring. It was framed with ideas like: Could a wrestler defeat a kickboxer? Could a martial artist defeat a sumo wrestler? It was unrefined, unedited, and unruly. Peter Hess, in the *Willamette Sports Law Journal,* documents its most shocking statement: "Each match will run until there is a designated winner by means of knockout, surrender, doctor's intervention or death."[69]

"The UFC promoted itself as a blood sport with few rules or safety protections for fighters . . . This emphasis on violent brutal contests eventually backfired."[70] The popularity of the events became well-known, and the media started covering this "new" phenomenon. "Newspapers and television shows started covering the story of the UFC, with its popularity being written as the latest sign of a decadent society."[71] With grotesque and vicious attacks in the first five UFC events taking place, the backlash of the situation met its most formidable foe in the political arena. It was almost knocked out in its infamous infancy.

"The key was political pressure causing, one-by-one, almost all the key cable systems to pull the shows, killing the key pay-per-view revenue stream."[72]

The greatest political foe to UFC was none other than presidential candidate John McCain. Senator McCain attacked the UFC with such force that it almost ceased to exist. After seeing a UFC match on video, he went into action sending a letter to all fifty governors of the United States to have it banned. He defined it as "human cockfighting" and a brutal blood sport "that should not be allowed to take place anywhere in the U.S."[73]

By December, 1995, thirty-six states had banned MMA fights. John McCain appeared to be the moral conscience needed to eradicate it. He put tremendous pressure on those companies broadcasting the events, with the desired results. He was dubbed the greatest foe of Ultimate Fighting Championship.

Refusing to submit, UFC began to go on the offensive. Though fledgling for a time with a change of ownership, it sought to overhaul its image. It survived in less regulated areas. Rather than run in defeat away from its greatest foe, it sought to embrace the very things it lacked. It became "refined," "respectable," and regulated.

It was hard for John McCain, who himself was a lightweight boxer, to maintain his footing in the battle because it became clear that he was attacking one combat sport while embracing another. True, boxing was regulated, but its legacy left it vulnerable.

"*The Velazquez Fatality Collection of Boxing Injuries* estimates that 1,358 professional boxers officially died from injuries in the ring during the 20th century, and that 112 fighters have died between 2000 and 2011. A report in the journal *Neuroscience* estimated that since the year 1900, on average, 10 boxers died from ring injuries each year."[74] The American Public Health Association called upon "the legislative and executive branches of governments at the national, state, and local levels to act to ban boxing in their jurisdictions" as early as 1985.[75]

It has been argued that Mixed Martial Arts is actually safer than boxing. Boxing has many more rounds than MMA, subjecting a boxer to more blows to the head over a sustained period of time. During the time that John McCain fought against it, no MMA fighter had actually died. Though it was only a matter of time before this claim could no longer be cited. To further weaken McCain's stance against the UFC, it was reported that he actually sat ringside during a boxing match that ended with one combatant dying in the hospital. This tragic event took place in a venue strikingly named Caesars Palace.

"Ironically, Senator McCain is an avid boxing fan and . . . sat ringside at the 'Ruelas vs. Garcia' Super Featherweight title bout. Jimmy Garcia died from injuries sustained in that bout. Luke O'Brien, a San Francisco-based reporter, described one perspective of the Senator's anti-UFC position: 'MMA supporters accused McCain, who once watched a boxer die in the ring but remained a loyal fan of the sweet science, of hypocrisy.'"[76]

Since then, UFC has apparently grown up. McCain's pressure drove it into the arms of regulation boards and committees. Its brutality is now sanctioned. Ancient Pankration has found acceptance once again. Peter Hess, writing in the *Willamette Sports Law Journal* in 2007, states, "The majority of states have approved MMA competitions. Reputable studies show that MMA is far safer than the well-established sport of boxing. Essentially, MMA is no longer a fighting spectacle. The sport of Pankration has come full circle; in time, it will find its way back home to the Olympics."[77]

McCain may have been personally satisfied that he brought UFC to become "safer," and yet his attempts to stamp it out all but failed. The irony continues, as the president of the UFC, Dana White, stated, "I consider John McCain the guy who started the UFC."[78]

BOXING AND THE ENLIGHTENMENT

"In 393 A.D., during the Roman gladiator period, boxing was abolished due to excessive brutality. It was not until the late 17th Century where boxing re-surfaced in London."[79] The Enlightenment (c. 1685-1815) in Europe was a time when humanity sought to throw off traditional structures and unquestioning allegiance to political and ecclesiastical authority. Human reason was supposed to be posited against Divine revelation.

For many, the idea was that man could rationalize all of life through science and philosophy. The Scriptures did not forbid man to think, but man often used God-given authority to prevent thought. The result was, for many, the throwing off of the Scripture and its truths in order to allow man to become all he could be.

No longer bound to glorify the Creator, people now used Humanism to glorify and deify humanity. This often resulted in bloody revolutions and wars. Who now would be the ultimate authority? The problem was not that reason and revelation could not co-exist in harmony, but that a reaction against suppression led to other forms of suppression because the balance had not been maintained. Beginning around the late 1600s, there was not only a human pursuit of knowledge, but also a call to return to the classics of the ancient past.

"The civilizations of ancient Greece and Rome formed both a common background and a major source of inspiration to Enlightenment thinkers and artists. The dominant culture of the Enlightenment was rooted in the classics . . ."[80] Humanity sought to rediscover the golden age of the past. The classics of Greece and Rome were hailed as the fount to which all civilized humanity should return. This movement extended its influence to a new generation of enlightened thinkers of the seventeenth century. These ideas influenced Darwin's grandfather, Erasmus Darwin (1731-1802), who was called a free-thinker. Darwin himself was deeply impacted by him and carried on the Humanist tradition.

During the Enlightenment, the clash of worldviews between Humanism and Christianity began. This clash continues down to this very day. Humanism elevates man without seeing any need to rely upon God for man's inherent worth. Not every humanist was an atheist, but deism was a step away from a personal God to Whom one was directly accountable. For many, God was impersonal and aloof. He may have been the first Cause, but He was distant and disconnected with the world. The Bible, claiming to be the Word of God, was rejected and replaced by the word of man.

The new thinking also challenged social norms. "During the Age of Enlightenment, Europeans took a keen interest in recovering the knowledge and traditions of antiquity. Such curiosity brought with it a revived interest in boxing, especially in England, the true birthplace of modern prize fighting."[81]

The resurfacing of boxing and its rise in the following centuries was not a coincidence. Much like Pankration, it was practiced in isolation; but when the time was right for a segment of society to embrace it, the struggle for recognition and regulation began. In all its complexities, history continues to repeat itself.

"By the 16th century, British boxing's Greek origins had been largely forgotten and if the sport was considered at all it was grouped with other rowdy rural pastimes, such as cockfighting and bear-baiting; all were outlawed under the Puritan government of Cromwell."[82] The evolution into boxing as we see it today again began in its infancy. It also faced resistance in England. The first account of a bare-knuckle fight in England was in the year 1681 in the *London Protestant Mercury*.

Though being illegal, the first boxing champion to emerge in England was James Figg in 1719. As it is now, so it was then that death was not unknown in the ring. Therefore, a series of rules began to be formulated to protect the fighters. "Rule changes in British boxing took into account not only shifts in societal norms but the inescapable fact that the sport was illegal."[83] The changes in social norms did not exclude the influence of Christianity. "Despite the change to the Queensberry rules, boxing was losing the social acceptability it had gained in England—partly because of changing middle-class values and an Evangelical religious revival intensely concerned about sinful pastimes."[84]

An example of this religious fervor is found within the pages of one of the best-selling books of all time. Charles Sheldon's fiction book, *In His Steps,* sold more than thirty million copies since it was first published in 1896.[85] It was the best-selling book in the Unites States for sixty years, only second to the Bible.[86] One section highlights the refusal of a newspaper editor to print the results of a prize fight:

> "Do you mean that the paper is to go to press without a word of the prize fight in it?"

> "Yes, that's what I mean."

> "But it's unheard of."

> "Clark, if Christ was editor of a daily paper, do you honestly think He would print three columns and a half of prize fight in it?"

> "No, I don't suppose He would . . . To succeed in the newspaper business we have to conform to the custom and the recognized methods of society. We can't do as we would in an ideal world."[87]

Boxing continued to fight for its own survival, being viewed by many as something from the barbaric past. It was outlawed in England and throughout much of the United States. This continued in fits and starts, even into the early 1900s. *William Blackstone's Commentaries on the Laws of England* (1765–69) stated its "unlawfulness" in his chapter on homicide. "And so are boxing and sword playing, the succeeding amusement of their posterity; and if a knight in the former case, or a gladiator in the latter, be killed, such killing is felony of manslaughter."[88] Interestingly, it was only the king who could lawfully allow such events where the killing would not be homicide. Blackstone cites Athens' and Rome's state-sanctioned *pancratium* to support the king's authority to do so.

Another example of its illegality is the Massachusetts State Supreme Court's 1876 ruling, which states, "Prize-fighting, boxing matches, and encounters of that kind, serve no useful purpose, tend to breaches of peace, and are unlawful even when entered into by agreement and without anger or mutual ill will."[89]

Christianity's impact on society still had tremendous sway. Yet its influence within this realm began to wane, often from within. "Up until 1920, prize-fighting was in a period of flux, legal in some places and not in others. The brutality of the sport did not concern the states; it was boxing's connection with gambling and corruption which had government officials keeping it at bay."[90] Its acceptance into the Olympics came around the same time.

"Boxing made its Olympic debut at the Games of the III Olympiad in St. Louis in 1904. In Stockholm in 1912, boxing was not on the program, as Swedish law prohibited its practice. Since then, boxing has been on the program of every edition of the Games."[91] By the early twentieth century, boxing was fully accepted as a sport regulated at the state level in the USA and almost globally. The fight was over. The battle to have boxing as a "respectable sport" took the same course that was followed by the UFC many decades later.

Sanctioning bodies and commissions were set up to regulate the sport and enforce the rules set out. State by state, the acceptance grew, until the tide was finally turned. Boxing was here to stay. Boxing, as we know it today, is accepted globally. The stage was now set for Pankration to make its return as well. Its acceptance has not taken centuries but just decades to reach a similar acceptance as its forerunner. Humanism's return to the ancient past is accelerating and gaining momentum for the future. It can be clearly seen as being in full flight. It is more sophisticated, more dazzling, but no less dangerous.

THE VOICE OF CONSCIENCE

It was May 6, 1995, when Gabriel Ruelas put on his boxing gloves and entered the boxing ring at Caesars Palace, Las Vegas, Nevada. He left as a man changed forever. He faced an unexpected opponent with whom it took eleven rounds before leaving him defeated.

Jimmy Garcia, a gritty Columbian boxer, stood his ground in a way that Ruelas did not expect. He punished him with blow after blow, and it took him a long time before Garcia succumbed. Professing Christian John McCain was seated with many cheering and elated fans. Garcia then collapsed, being carried out on a stretcher, and shuttled to the hospital.

When the champion finally found out the terrible news, he rushed to see Garcia. "Ruelas and his wife were in a hospital waiting room feeling exponential guilt."[92] What he saw next, he could not be prepared for. Ruelas stated, "His [Garcia's] lips were swollen; his head was swollen . . . I didn't think he was going to make it."[93]

The inner torment the seasoned boxing champ felt swirled into a cyclone of confusion. He believed it wasn't his fault, but he kept feeling it was. People gave reasons why he shouldn't feel that way. Yet, it was he who had punched him. The images of the match haunted him, and his mind wouldn't let up. Garcia was dead.

Ruelas was unsure if he would ever box again. In time, he returned to the ring a changed man. He would fight, but with the intention of not hurting his opponent—a mixture that ultimately undid his career. Ruelas says, "It was very traumatic. Psychologically it just destroyed me."[94]

As hard as he tried, he could not be the same person he was. He was wracked with guilt. "I didn't want to hurt anyone anymore and in boxing you have to have that. I started feeling bad for fighters and when you do that its [sic] time to get out."[95] After a later bout, he recounts, "I was thinking about Jimmy and I paid for it. I could not get him out of my mind. When I looked across the ring I saw Jimmy."[96]

Years later, the confusion still resounded in the words of Ruelas. The fact is that Ruelas' God-given conscience had declared it was his fault. He had, for money and fame, taken the life of another individual. No amount of comfort or consoling could change that fact. He was feeling guilty because in God's eyes, he truly was guilty. He had shed the blood of a man who was created in the image of God. It mattered little to his conscience that it was just a sport.

He knew and believed that as a boxer, he shouldn't feel this way, but there was a higher law, buried deep within, that was burning into his soul. Even though he didn't want to believe it, nor did all the cheering fans, he had done something terribly wrong. Ruelas was driven to donate large amounts of money to the Garcia family "and yet he could still not unclamp the guilt."[97]

Ruelas was not the only one who suffered from a guilty conscience as endowed by God. In the same location, years earlier, a nationally televised event at Caesars Palace again snuffed out a life in front of a cheering crowd. Ray "Boom Boom" Mancini took on a ferocious Korean opponent by the name of Kim Duk-koo.

Kim wrote on the lampshade in his hotel room before the match, "Kill or be killed." After the fight, Mancini, the hailed victor, was publicly introduced by Frank Sinatra in none other than the Circus Maximus Showroom.[98] The elation did not last long as the devastation of the match left Mancini riddled with guilt for decades. The tragedy reached far outside the ring. Kim's own mother committed suicide, as well as referee Richard Green, as a result of the fight.

Mancini was able to meet Kim's son some thirty years later. In the article titled, "A Step Back: Families Continue to Heal After 30 years After Title Fight Between Ray Mancini and Duk-koo Kim," Mancini says, "I felt guilt about what happened for a long time . . . I felt guilty because of your mother. I felt guilty that you never met your father."[99]

Changes to the number of rounds in a boxing match took place in an attempt to limit the carnage. For those of us who profess Christ as Lord, are we going to mourn the loss of life as a tragic death in sport, or are we going to mourn the death of those created in God's image? Are we going to agree that these were just accidents, or are we going to recognize the internal guilty verdict against these two men?

The only freedom from such guilt is found in the One Whose blood was shed for such sins. Is it not tragic that our Western society has endorsed such events and that professing Christian John McCain was present during the bout which took the life of someone created in the image of God?

Yet, in spite of it all, Senator McCain did not change directions. He actually warmed up to the idea of the UFC because it was now a regulated sport and not merely a spectacle. Should the name of Christ be associated with such blood sports, or should Christianity take an opposing stance? Does the blood spilled on the cross speak against the blood spilled in the ring? Should those who are blood-bought be opposed to blood sports?

The book *The Lure of the Arena* suggests the need for a call within the Church to reexamine its participation in popular culture. "The gulf that apparently separates the Roman arena spectator from the consumer of violent modern entertainment is thus not quite so wide as it might first appear."[100] Thus, it is for good reason that even historians hesitate to say that we are different. The truth is that there is not just a little part of them in us; they are our relatives. Darwin did not know this; but through his book *The Descent of Man*, he was espousing not just his faith about how we all got here, but also the beginnings of the road back to Rome.

In his book, Darwin denounced Rome by stating, "How little the old Romans knew of it (sympathy) is shown by their abhorrent gladiatorial exhibitions."[101] Yet whether he intended or not, his new view of humanity undermined the very truths that brought an end to the abhorrent games. Not only that, but his worldview could lead the world, if not checked, back into the abyss in which Rome had found itself.

Would we not be as guilty as Darwin by elevating ourselves above the Romans? Could not an ideology of superiority sweep the globe and plunge the world into an even more sophisticated version of the Roman Empire, with its first principles coming from Darwin and not God? If we take the Word of God seriously, the human heart, unchecked by God's power, will do it again.

CHAPTER 4

BLOOD-BOUGHT VS. BLOOD SPORT

*And I don't think there is anything purer, than two guys in a cage . . . just to see
which man is better. And as a Pastor and Bible teacher I think that God made
man masculine . . . That is just the way men are made, so we either allow that in a
way which is violence and inappropriate which a lot of guys do through criminal
activity or we put it together as a viable legitimate sport. Let men be men.*

—Pastor Mark Driscoll,
Former Lead Pastor, Mars Hill Church[102]

"HARD PUNCHES!" HE SHOUTED FROM the sidelines. "Finish the fight! To
the head! To the head!"[103] At the time of the article, Pastor Renken, church
founder and leader of an evangelical fight ministry encouraged one of his
team to end it. This was at a Mixed Martial Arts event called Cage Assault. The
irony in the *New York Times* article became clear, as a prayer meeting one hour
earlier had Pastor Renken praying that they would be representatives of God.

But "a member of his flock who had bowed his head was now unleashing
a torrent of blows on an opponent, and Mr. Renken was offering guidance
that was not exactly prayerful."[104] The evangelistic outreach didn't exactly end
in victory. One potential convert, who had lost his bout by being choked out,
didn't head back with the rest of Renken's fight team, but headed out to the
bars in Memphis' night life.

The "sport" of Mixed Martial Arts has not only entered stadiums around North America and the globe, but its influence and fame have now been embraced by many within the visible Christian community. Its acceptance in various churches has ranged from being actively embraced by the leadership to being quietly accepted by the flock. Many Christians are simply uninformed about what is transpiring.

Those who have embraced this openly have even built ministries focused on MMA. Their goal is to bring the message of Jesus as a fighter, Who never gave up. In MMA, the action of tapping means to give up. Thus the slogan "Jesus did not tap" has become popular in many circles. The idea that we are to "fight the good fight" has led a number to portray Jesus as the warrior Savior, compatible with Ultimate Fighting. One example is the "Fight Pastor," Brandon Beals. He hearkens to such ideas as "predestined to fight" saying, "But what led me to Christ was that Jesus was a fighter."[105]

These might appear to be extreme fringe churches; yet its acceptance may be a surprise. The documentary *Fight Church* highlights leadership within evangelical communities that use MMA to spread the Gospel. "In fact, the film estimates that there are currently over 700 churches with MMA ministries in the US."[106] As MMA gains traction and interest, so the burgeoning growth within the sport has many within congregations across North America watching Pay-per-view events on Saturday nights—just hours before heading off to church the next morning.

The portrayal of Jesus Christ is of a tough Man Who went to the cross and refused to back down while suffering unimaginable pain. It is identifying with the pain, struggle, apparent defeat, and ultimate victory of Christ that should guide the Christian man. The leaders within the documentary "spend the bulk of their interviews advocating not only for the compatibility of Christianity and MMA, but also suggesting a cultural need for such relations."[107]

In recent years, more and more leadership have taken the position that Western Christianity has become feminized. The need of the Church is to elevate masculine Christianity in order to combat its feminization. The way to do this is to promote tough men, ready to fight.

Ryan Dobson, whose father founded Focus on the Family, states: "We've raised a generation of little boys."[108] An avid MMA supporter, he is for taking back ground in the cultural war for lost souls and feminized Christians.

A similar movement in the late 1800s also sought to turn the tide of feminization within the church. History, again, has a way of repeating itself. The name across its banner was "Muscular Christianity." It sought to promote men being men through encouraging weightlifting and sport. "In the latter half of the nineteenth century, boxing found advocates within the 'Muscular Christianity' movement which saw sports as a way to increase not only a man's physical, but also his moral strength. Many churches ran their own gyms and supported fighters."[109]

A new muscular Christianity aligning itself with Pankration has arisen, seeking to embed MMA and Christianity into its theology. The new heroes in this movement are none other than MMA and UFC fighters themselves. Many UFC fighters have promoted themselves as Christians. The term *Christian* in today's world is undoubtedly broad, but for many, any star or political leader who calls him or herself a Christian is all that is required. The cultural trends are seen as a way to promote and legitimize Christianity. Jesus did not tap-out (quit), and neither should you.

Reports of Christian influence within UFC started close to its inception and have continued. In UFC 3, Kimo, a fighter, carried a wooden cross toward the Octagon; painted on it were the words "JESUS LOVES YOU." Another vivid portrayal of this was photographed within the Octagon itself. Rich Franklin, who has professed to be a born-again Christian, is pictured bowing and praying after pummeling his opponent.

Perhaps many Christian ministries are clamoring to make gains through the popular rise of MMA and UFC. Yet the UFC is not clamoring to return the favor. UFC President Dana White told the fighters that they should keep

Jesus out. After knocking out his opponent, Yoel Romero, who wore John 3:16 on his headband, made post-fight statements about the USA returning to Jesus. Dana responded, "You just won the biggest fight of your career, America doesn't want to hear your thoughts on Jesus, keep that stuff at home."[110] Dana, reportedly an atheist, wanted him to talk only about the fight. "It's awesome you love Jesus. Love Jesus all you want. You just don't have to do it publicly."[111]

SHALT THOU PUNCH THY NEIGHBOR IN THE FACE?

The uncomfortable question of biblical Christianity and its compatibility with MMA will undoubtedly continue endlessly. Various opinions have surfaced. For many like Pastor Beals, MMA is truly the way to connect with Jesus as a Man. Christian faith is strengthened through learning the disciplines and combative ideas of the sport. When asked how the brutal violence of UFC can mesh with Christianity, he states, "I'm not going to answer that in Bible verses."[112]

For others, MMA is a teaching tool to be used, on occasion, with the idea that Scripture does not explicitly condemn it. While they do not defend it nor publicly endorse it, their silence portrays to the congregation that though perhaps not desirable, neither is it to be condemned.

It is interesting that Tertullian would face the same reasoning by individuals in his day, saying that because Scripture does not exactly state, "Thou shalt not look on combat," it was doubtful of being sin.[113] This line of reasoning is very dangerous and faulty. Just because the Bible does not say, "Thou shalt not perform an abortion," it is still contrary to biblical teaching. He also would oppose gladiatorial bouts by saying the Bible forbids murder. Tertullian would then go on to reference Psalm 1:1 as applying to spectators: "How blessed is the man who does not walk in counsel of the wicked, Nor stand in the path of sinners, Nor sit in the seat of scoffers!"

Still others take the stand that if two men or women are foolish enough to subject themselves to such abuse, then we needn't care. Ignoring it as irrelevant is the best course of action. Yet perhaps a focus on history would be helpful in realizing that we do not exist in a vacuum. Choices made in society do not stay in isolation.

Finally, the author himself would suggest to all Scripture is not silent on such matters and individuals do engage in things which, even though there is mutual consent, ought not to be. It takes only the putting together of the first principles of God and His commandments to determine it is so. Scripture may not specifically mention every sin, but every sin is within the purview of Scripture.

One former MMA fighter, Scott "Bam Bam" Sullivan, "eventually realized a discordance between his newfound religion and his participation in combat sports. 'I'm conflicted,' he tells the camera, as he owns an MMA gym and works on a Ph.D. in the philosophy of religion. Christianity and sport fighting are 'incompatible.'"[114]

The most obvious place to begin is with the very words of Jesus Himself. "Blessed are the peacemakers, for they shall be called sons of God" (Matt. 5:9). No one upholding Jesus as Savior would object to this. Yet, the argument goes that in *sports*, it is permissible to fight. By the sport being sanctioned and controlled, these activities are legitimized. This is despite the fact that if the fight took place on the sidewalk, both parties would go to jail. It is believed that if something is called a sport, somehow, it is "sanctified."

The "sport" is now set apart to a new level which cannot be condemned. It is no longer criminal violence but legitimate. Terminology is actually interchanged to cover sin. Violence as entertainment is now called a sport; murder is called an accident; ungodly anger is called high emotions; enjoying brutality is called enjoying the skill; human sacrifice is called the risk in combat. The apostle Peter states, "*Act as* free men, and do not use your freedom as a covering for evil, but *use it* as bondslaves of God" (1 Peter 2:16).

ANSWERING WITH BIBLE VERSES

The nature of God is that He is Love. When He shows His wrath, it is a judicial action against sin. The love of Jesus was a redeeming love. His blood was shed on the cross to pay for the very evil that people have perpetrated against each other. His strength lay in the very fact that He did not strike back. Isaiah states of the coming Messiah, "Because He had done no violence, Nor was there any deceit in His mouth" (Isa. 53:9b).

MMA is all about violence, and it is opposed to the life of Christ. Jesus came for the purpose of bringing peace between God and man. This peace would then overflow into mankind being able to have peace with each other. The writer to the Hebrews says, "Pursue peace with all men, and the sanctification without which no one will see the Lord" (Heb. 12:14). We are to live as Jesus lived. He is the Prince of Peace.

Was Jesus tough? Anyone who can fast for forty days, walk countless miles, and endure the cross without sinning has amazing spiritual and physical stamina. There is no doubt that for Jesus to endure what He did, even in the last week of His life, He was physically fit. But Jesus did not take on the tough guy persona. Children ran to Him; women felt safe around Him; and He was completely pure in word and deed. In contrast, sinful humanity, throughout its history, has had no lack of fighting; it has lacked the ability to love as God loves. It takes no supernatural power to strike someone in the face. On the contrary, to love your enemies with the love of God, we must have the empowerment of Jesus Christ Himself. Jesus said, "For apart from Me you can do nothing" (John 15:5b).

One of the greatest arguments against fighting in sports comes down to what happens within the heart. It has already been affirmed that every human being is created in the image of God. To murder an individual is tantamount to attacking God Himself.

The Gospel writer John consistently reinforces the themes of love versus hatred. In First John, he states, "Everyone who hates his brother is a murderer;

and you know that no murderer has eternal life abiding in him" (1 John 3:15). The apostle Paul says, "Love does no wrong to a neighbor" (Rom. 13:10a).

Sullivan, a former MMA fighter-turned-critic, states, "Christianity is about love . . . and 'this ain't love' . . . cage fighting is about hating one another."[115] Thus, "Christian mixed martial artists are a walking contradiction, evidence of religion gone awry."[116]

There are those who may try to redefine love and hate, but changing definitions doesn't change the truth. It doesn't take a lot of research to find out what is really going on inside a fighter. Jesus said, "For the mouth speaks out of that which fills the heart" (Matt. 12:34b).

One of the greatest rivalries in UFC history was between two former heavyweight champions, Frank Mir and Brock Lesnar. In a radio interview, Mir stated how many fighters use "public relations" language because they are worried about being politically correct. Mir would have none of that. He stated, "I want to fight Lesnar. I hate who he is as a person. I want to break his neck in the ring. I want him to be the first person that dies due to Octagon-related injuries. That's what is going through my mind."[117] Lesnar would return in kind, saying he was counting the days until he got to murder Mir.

Mir and Lesnar are not the only ones to have verbally expressed their murderous hatred. B.J. Penn stated via video to Georges St-Pierre, "Georges, I'm going to go to the death. I'm going to try to kill you and I'm not joking about this."[118] Kenny Florian turned some heads when he said from the ring to B.J. Penn, "I consider you a master, and its [sic] time to kill that master."[119]

It is truly unconvincing to argue that fighters do not have hateful feelings against each other when they enter the ring. This "sport," as it is declared, is completely based on violently subduing an opponent. Death can be a reality in the ring, and the threat of it is always present, even for the best of fighters. If love is an action word, then hate is as well. No one can desire to and purposely beat, punch, kick, choke, and cause brain damage to an opponent and claim to love him. This claim is an oxymoron.

Sam Vasquez, Michael Kirkham, Tyrone Mims, Booto Guylain, and Donshay White are remembered for their deaths within sanctioned MMA events. The claim that MMA has caused no deaths has been vanquished forever.

Up until the date of this writing, no one has died in the most professional level of MMA, UFC. This claim, though, can no longer be made for MMA as a whole. As is true with any sport, it is the professionals who have access to the best medical help and attention (as they did in ancient Rome). It is not surprising that the fourteen deaths that have occurred are at its lower ranks. Some fights have been sanctioned; others have not; but the final result has been the same—the death of a young man.

Is it not interesting that before the two fighters enter the ring, murder (through hatred) has already taken place? The very fact that individuals would enter into a ring in order to maim another into submission totally contradicts what Christianity is all about. The very fact that the media picks up on such contradictions should give even the most ardent supporter of "Christian" MMA pause for thought. They know it; why don't we?

GOD HATES VIOLENCE

Advocates for CMMA (Christian Mixed Martial Arts) will often appeal to the Old Testament to support their case. There is no doubt that there are many accounts of war and of bloodshed within its pages. In the Old Testament, it states there is "a time for war and a time for peace" (Eccl. 3:8b). We also need to remember that the Bible often tells things the way they happened—such as Joab's murder of Abner—but does not sanction it.

King David, a man of war and bloodshed, wrote a stunning account of the distinctions Scripture declares. David himself saw a difference between his life as a warrior and the love of violence in a society. Psalm eleven sets the context by revealing the Lord as being a refuge against the wicked man's attempt to murder the righteous. In verse three, it states, "If the foundations are destroyed, What can the righteous do?"

This Psalm that talks about the foundations of a nation being destroyed through evil, leaving the righteous little recourse, also states: "The LORD tests the righteous and the wicked, And the one who loves violence His soul hates" (Psalm 11:5). The context of this verse resides in the realm of society: its decay and the rise of violence and wickedness. We will discuss the definition of violence in the chapter to come. Yet William MacDonald states of God, "He hates all evildoers—a truth that punctures the prevalent myth that God is all love and therefore incapable of hatred . . . Although God is infinite love, His soul hates men who practice violence."[120]

If a nation has been eroded to the extent that the righteous heritage has been attacked and destroyed, the saints are limited in effecting its reversal. In the same passage, it is a people who are in love with violence that will bring God's judgment. This should cause our minds to hearken back to what happened in the days of Noah. It was because "the earth was corrupt before God, and the earth was filled with violence" (Gen. 6:11) that He would cause the global flood.

UFC is brutal violence, and those who watch as fans love it. This is a dangerous mixture for professing Christians to endorse or in which to participate. "For our struggle [lit. wrestling] is not against flesh and blood but against the rulers, against the powers, against the world forces of this darkness" (Eph. 6:12).

Augustine called the gladiatorial games "cruel and deadly shows," also mentioning how the demons delighted in such displays.[121] Theophilus, the early church writer states, "We are forbidden even to witness shows of gladiators, so that we do not become partakers and abettors of murder. Nor may we see the other spectacles, lest our eyes and our ears be defiled . . . "[122] Theophilus brings up a powerful argument. We need to be reminded again that we can live vicariously through others and participate in the evil of others we observe. *Vicarious* means that which is "experienced or realized through imaginative or sympathetic participation in the experience of another."[123] Many people live their dreams through their children, movie stars, or sports heroes.

If we can participate through our emotions—as one can commit murder and adultery in their heart (1 John 3:15; Matt. 5:21-22, 27-28)—surely we can be defiled by choosing to watch and hear evil entertainment. What would the early Church say to us in our day? Perhaps one may think there is no relationship between then and now, or perhaps not even care. Would they be concerned about the direction many in the modern Church are going? Would they speak out, even if the gladiators of our day are not as extreme as they were in their day—yet?

THE MMA CULTURE

If we look at Mixed Martial Arts as a whole, the culture itself should raise serious concern. Leaders of Christian ministries are proclaiming that men ought to be masculine, bold, and warriors. They are to fight the good fight of faith, boldly bringing forth the Gospel of Christ. Yet they lead them to a place of tremendous vulnerability, where men consistently fall. The oft-quoted saying against immorality offers a blistering warning to all men: "If you think you can't fall into sexual sin, then you are godlier than David, stronger than Samson and wiser than Solomon."[124]

The culture of UFC and MMA is not only verbally and physically destructive, but the displays of women and men as sex objects are an integral part of every match. Women are immodestly and sensually paraded before the eyes of the crowd. Blood lust and sexual lust are in full throttle. Self-defense is called for by the apostle John when he says, "Little children, guard yourselves from idols" (1 John 5:21).

Sexual sin, throughout Scripture, has taken down the mightiest of men, and yet, somehow, MMA is thought to help sanctify the Christian man. How can these co-exist? How could married men (or single) sit and watch these women and avoid lust? Paul commands, "But put on the Lord Jesus Christ, and make no provision for the flesh in regard to *its* lusts" (Rom. 13:14). How honoring is it to one's wife to watch such displays? Jesus declared, "But I say to you that everyone who looks at a woman with lust for her has already committed adultery with her in his heart" (Matt. 5:28).

Solomon had firsthand knowledge of the dangers of adultery as experienced by his father, David. He also knew personally, all too well, of the ability of idolatrous women to turn his own heart from God. He warns, "Watch over your heart with all diligence, For from it *flow* the springs of life" (Prov. 4:23). Interestingly enough, this admonition is four verses away from his great discourse on warning men against the wiles of the adulteress.

THE BLOOD-BOUGHT

The tensions of living in a world with so many moral choices and differing opinions is that we can come to the point where we believe we can't find the truth of the matter. The voices of the crowd can drown out our sense of the true path. "What about this?" "What about that?" Questions are useful in seeking to be consistent in a position; but when they are used solely to deflect one from the teachings of Scripture or the purity of a godly life, they lead astray. Not one of us knows all the answers, except the Lord, "in whom are hidden all the treasures of wisdom and knowledge" (Col. 2:3). We must use the Word of God as our guide.

Ultimately, each individual is accountable before the Lord, for He knows each heart. Paul talks about how "bodily discipline is only of little profit, but godliness is profitable for all things" (1 Tim. 4:8), even fitness. Discerning sin is actually where the training must take place. The writer to the Hebrews calls believers to train and practice for the mature Christian life. "But solid food is for the mature, who because of practice have their senses trained to discern good and evil" (Heb. 5:14). This tells us that it takes diligence and maturity to discern the nuances of sin and the mystery of lawlessness in our day.

Even the apostle Paul declared, in a very succinct way, how the confession and the conduct of the blood-bought must be in harmony. It is a serious warning that must be heeded by all of us. In the same letter that Paul writes of Demas, a close friend and companion in ministry, abandoning him for the love of the world, he states, "Nevertheless, the firm foundation of God stands, having this seal, 'The Lord knows those who are His,' and, 'Everyone who names the name of the Lord is to abstain from wickedness'" (2 Tim. 2:19).

Jesus Himself affirms this demand in His judgment toward those whose confession, "Lord, Lord," would contradict their lifestyle. "And then I will declare to them, 'I never knew you; DEPART FROM ME, YOU WHO PRACTICE LAWLESSNESS'" (Matt. 7:23).

The prophet Isaiah points us to the path to walk while dwelling with God, Who "is a consuming fire" (Heb. 12:29). "Who among us can live with the consuming fire? . . . He who walks righteously and speaks with sincerity . . . He who stops his ears from hearing about bloodshed And shuts his eyes from looking upon evil" (Isa. 33:14-15).

CHAPTER 5

THE CONCUSSION CRISIS

"PRAY FOR CHAD" WAS THE call that went out as Chad Stover was fighting for his life in hospital. Chad, a likable sixteen-year-old, was looking forward to his birthday and, having made the playoffs, was enjoying the thought of defeating the football team favored to win "Sacred Heart." He suited up but was carried off the field, having to be airlifted to the hospital.

It was a routine hit, given by Chad himself, that caused his head to hit the thigh of an oncoming player and smash into the ground. Chad made his way to the sideline. Everything appeared normal, but what was happening inside Chad's brain was anything but normal. It caused his legs to buckle under him just six minutes before the end of the game. His parents rushed frantically onto the field, and both teams gathered around him for prayer, entreating God to save his life.

As he lay on the field, a tear trickled down his cheek. His mother later stated, "He has so many different injuries going on in that beautiful head of his." My own tears flow as I write these words. Chad was diagnosed with catastrophic head injuries. The *Time* magazine cover story featured a picture of Chad with the title, "He Died Playing This Game. Is Football Worth It?"[125] A year after this article was published, seven high-school football players in the United States died due to their injuries within a seven-week period.[126] Author Sean Gregory states it as "the tragic risks of an American obsession."[127]

Modern technology and research on brain trauma has caused an explosion of media and political attention. No longer is society able to excuse itself with, "We just didn't know." Stories regarding concussions in hockey, football, boxing, and mixed martial arts have become commonplace, due to the growing studies that show long-term brain impairment. The "punch drunk" phrase was recognized back in the 1920s, but now we understand more about what is actually taking place and its specific link to sports.

The issue comes down to the three pounds of fat called "the brain." It is one of the most amazing and mysterious creations of God. We are still just beginning to understand the effects of head trauma in the realm of concussions. Yet one may wonder how many studies are needed to reveal what we should intuitively know by now. Repeated head trauma leads to greater brain damage.

The spark that ignited the growing firestorm was none other than a football star, whose nickname sadly did not stand up to reality. The Pittsburgh Steelers sensation Mike "Iron" Webster died literally a broken man. The seventeen-year veteran and star, who led the Steelers to four NFL Super Bowl victories, was left unable to carry on a normal conversation. He lived with depression, fits of rage, memory loss, and a litany of other problems. His wife recounts him taking a knife in a rage and cutting up all of his football pictures. Before his death, the superstar was actually living in his truck.

A doctor named Dr. Bennet Omalu was the one who carried out Mike's autopsy. His findings presented evidence for a disease that was insidious. His discovery of a link between head trauma and football ignited a raging controversy and led to a confrontation with the National Football League. The book League of Denial "reveals how the NFL, over a period of nearly two decades, sought to cover up and deny mounting evidence of the connection between football and brain damage."[128]

Dr. Omalu was part of a drama that challenged not only the secrets of men's minds, but also their hearts. In the years to follow, decisions may not be based so much on what the science tells us, but on the level of tolerance society has for accepting head trauma casualties. More studies will give us increased knowledge, but will it change hearts? Will the years ahead reveal that the "American obsession" did, indeed, skew our view of what science, doctors, and even Scripture tell us?

CTE

Dr. Bennet Omalu observed and brought to light a hidden disease that has rocked the sports world. CTE (Chronic Traumatic Encephalopathy) is a disease that develops over time due to concussions from constant blows to the head. When the head is hit, the brain bounces off the skull. One study concluded that "American footballers sustain a blow to the head equivalent to a severe car crash in every game."[129] Repetitive head trauma causes a build-up of proteins in the brain, and degeneration occurs. For some sports stars, the "analysis of their brain tissue revealed the presence of a protein usually seen in the brains of elderly people with dementia, but almost never in normal middle-aged men."[130]

According to a study published in the 2017 *Journal of the American Medical Association*, "110 of 111 deceased NFL players had suffered from chronic traumatic encephalopathy," with repeated blows causing the worst damage.[131] Even prior to this study, revelations of the damage caused over forty-five hundred former NFL players to launch a class action suit against the NFL itself, contending that the league had willfully misled players regarding long-term head trauma.[132] Within the NFL Concussion Settlement, hundreds of millions of dollars have been awarded to former players.[133]

Concussion, a movie released in 2015, attempted to chronicle the battle a single doctor had in taking the National Football League head-on. Though a disappointment at the box office, the science it presented cannot be denied. Reporter Bill Plaschke sums up well CTE's relation to football: "All this affection for an ancient and brutal game of gladiators. We loudly cheer as they slowly die."[134]

The glaring pattern kept repeating in the form of sports stars and their loved ones suffering. There have been a long line of suicides from National Football League players who were struggling with depression. Dave Duerson, who played for the Chicago Bears football team, shot himself in the chest, requesting that his brain be studied. "The NFL fraternity has seen too many of its brothers take their lives in recent years—among them Dave Duerson, Ray Easterling, and Paul Oliver. There even have been incidents on the college level, such as Kosta Karageorge of Ohio State. Before shooting himself, Karageorge left a note for his mother, saying that his head was messed up from concussions."[135] One clue into these tragedies is that a man's brain development, which controls things like personality expression, cognitive thinking, and social behavior, can continue into the ages of twenty-nine to thirty.[136]

Historically, death can be traced back within football to its early years. In 1909, twenty-six people died in football games, mostly due to brutal violence during scrums. Massive changes overhauled the sport that was in danger of being banned. Author John Miller states, "There's this social and political movement that rises up to outlaw the sport. It's led by the president of Harvard and a number of other well-known figures. They equate football with homicide."[137]

It took President Teddy Roosevelt, whose own son was seriously injured in a game, to bring a massive overhaul to actually save the game. This is chronicled in Miller's *The Big Scrum: How Teddy Roosevelt Saved Football.* But despite the many changes and attempts to contain the damage, the carnage has continued in many forms. As often happens, it is the up-and-coming players who are most at risk. "Between 1982 and 2009 according to the National Center for Catastrophic Injury Research, *295 fatalities* directly or indirectly resulted from high-school football" (emphasis mine).[138]

The National Hockey League has also been involved in its own firestorm. Former player, fighter, and general manager Mike Milbury "citing the number of concussions resulting from the league's fisticuffs, particularly the staged version, conceded, 'The only reason we have fighting in the game is because we like it.'"[139]

In contrast, the Bible says love "does not rejoice in unrighteousness" (1 Cor. 13:6). In a fight against Corey Fulton, Don Sanderson, a senior player in the Single A League, shattered forever the myth that no one ever gets seriously hurt in hockey fights. Fulton—like boxers Ruelas and Mancini—has been haunted by being the reason for his opponent's death.[140] The hidden damage through CTE has also been exposed. Bob Probert, a famous brawler who played for the Detroit Red Wings, was found to have CTE after he died at the age of forty-five. The evidence is clear, but what are the barriers to definitive change that cloud the issue?

THE NATURE OF A SPORT

When we start to deal with sports like hockey and football, things can begin to get cloudy. For the sake of understanding the differences between sports and blood sports, we need to seek what the nature of a particular sport is. One example is hockey. For those who say fighting is just a part of hockey, we need to remember the obvious: the goal of hockey is to put the puck in the net. These games can even be played in a "non-contact" format. "Non-contact" doesn't mean there will never be contact between players, as two individuals going for the puck are sure to connect at times. The issue is they are going for the puck, not intentionally after each other.

Intentional crushing contact, headshots, and fighting ought to be banned and severely disciplined because of spiritual, moral, and health issues. Many continue to argue that fighting is a part of hockey, but the reality is, it can't be; *it is illegal.* That is like saying spearing and charging are a part of hockey. It cannot be; it is penalized. As Milbury admits, fighting is present and, in many ways, tolerated in hockey because people like it. The fans are the ones who pay the bills, and it is not going to change unless fans' and management's hearts change.

A second example is football. The goal of football is to get a touchdown. The essence of football itself can also be played in a "non-contact" way. Though tackle football is still very popular, there has been a shift to more children playing flag football in recent years.[141] After the death of seven high school football players in seven weeks, the American Pediatric Association gave a number of recommendations. We must remember that pediatrics means we are dealing with children. One recommendation was to properly train young people how to tackle without leading with the head; and the most extreme recommendation was *removing tackling from high school football altogether.*

The American Pediatric Society is actually recommending a ban on tackling for high school children. Many dismiss this as unacceptable and unrealistic, but is it?[142] The numbers show that not everyone is convinced that tackle football is a risk worth taking. One article titled, "Safety concerns prompt sharp drop in youth football participation," highlights the increased concerns.[143] Dr. Paul Echlin even states, "No child should be ethically allowed to participate in tackle football."[144] Hockey has seen increased calls to ban full-contact checking for youngsters as well.[145]

If it is unacceptable for many to take the violence out of children's football, which has killed numerous young people (see statistics above), there is no way our society will ever challenge the college and professional leagues. Full-contact football is what draws the crowds. The billion-dollar industry of the NFL is a huge driving force. The heart of the matter is that things are not going to change unless there is a change of heart.

CONSCIENCE SPEAKS

"LT, I will be back."

"Yeah, Joe, but not tonight."[146]

This was the exchange between Joe Theismann of the Washington Redskins and L.T. (Lawrence Taylor) of the New York Giants. The circumstances prompted the *Washington Post* to term it, "The Hit That No One Who Saw It Can Ever Forget."[147]

The date was November 18, 1985. Quarterback Joe Theismann was playing a strong game. The unfortunate toss back to him was anticipated by the Giants' defense. The routine tackle by Lawrence Taylor made Taylor's right knee slam into Theismann's leg, which buckled under the impact and resulted in a compound fracture.

> But anyone who knows the famous highlight remembers Taylor's mortified reaction to Theismann's injury. That has stuck with Theismann, too: When Taylor realizes how bad Theismann is injured, he leaps up to his feet, waves frantically to the sideline for trainers and medical personnel to rush onto the field, and then places both hands on his helmet as if to say "what have I done?"[148]

Theismann was wheeled off on a stretcher to the biggest standing ovation of his career. He never returned to the gridiron again.

The next day, Lawrence phoned Joe in the hospital to see how things were progressing. They have joked through the years with each other, but each of them have refused to watch the replay of what happened. Taylor states, "How I grew up was it's a gladiator sport," but both Super Bowl champs, as well as many who viewed the event, were touched by the stark reality of the situation.[149] What was witnessed that day jolted viewers to the realization that we are dealing with humans touched in conscience, rather than distant stars on a TV screen.

Another incident in the NFL some twenty-seven years later, however, might cause us to ask, "Has society continued to deteriorate in so short a time?" The date was October 7, 2012. The Kansas City Chiefs was playing the Baltimore Ravens. The Chiefs' fans had become increasingly agitated with the performance of quarterback Matt Cassel. An airplane was even sighted flying over Arrowhead Stadium calling for Cassel to be benched and the coach fired. It was also during this particular game that things finally reached the boiling point.

During the game, the unfortunate Matt Cassel was knocked unconscious, having been rocked by a hit while making his pass. Commentators and columnists alike were shocked when Kansas City Chiefs fans began to cheer. After the game, offensive tackle Eric Winston blasted his own fans with a fiery rebuke. "We are athletes, okay? We are athletes. We are not gladiators. This is not the Roman Coliseum . . . But when you cheer, when you cheer somebody getting knocked out, I don't care who it is, and it just so happened to be Matt Cassel—it's sickening. It's 100 percent sickening."[150]

There ensued a controversy as to how many people were actually cheering the injury. Whether it was seven hundred or seventy thousand, there was no doubt, even for the Baltimore Ravens, that Chiefs' fans had crossed the line. Winston summed it up by saying, "But we've got a lot of problems as a society if people think that's OK."[151]

One might think that a society where even the medical community is recommending banning contact in sports at the youth levels, where helmets and other protective gear are mandatory, would clearly see the issues surrounding boxing and MMA. The very purpose and nature of boxing and MMA is to *knock out* your opponent (i.e. inflict brain damage). This is contrary to the very thing most other sports are seeking to eradicate from junior to professional levels. MMA and its recent acceptance have now ramped everything up to a new level, which really shows how sickening and murky the issue is. This murkiness, however, serves their purpose: selling brutality.

A SOCIETY CONFLICTED

"You know it is probably more exciting to die in a competition than it is to die, you know, an old man peeing your pants in a bed somewhere."[152] These are striking words spoken by UFC color commentator, Joe Rogan, about the dangers of fighting in the Ultimate Fighting Championship. Rogan, like all of us, can be quite shortsighted when we don't understand the ramifications of our words. When someone dies in the ring, it affects family, children, and friends and has a host of other devastating consequences.

Jimmy Garcia left behind a wife and three small children. Do we take time to consider the tears shed by little girls who would never see their daddy again? Kim Duk-koo was killed while his little boy was unborn in his mother's womb. This young man never met his father. What kind of quality of life was left for them? Are we concerned about what was sacrificed? This also does not take into account the eternal destination of individuals. Is it not unfathomable that those who are blood-bought would be cheering, while a man or woman without Christ hits the canvas and is thrust toward an eternal Hell?

Jesus warned that every careless word would be brought into judgment. Rogan's words resonate with a careless attitude. Not surprisingly, a worldview that rejects the image of God in mankind and devalues human life elevates the reckless. Again, the weak, such as old men, are dishonored, while the strong are dispensable. The apostle Paul envisioned perilous times in the end. In the last times, even men, within the visible church but not of it, would be "lovers of self, lovers of money . . . unloving . . . brutal . . . treacherous, reckless, conceited, lovers of pleasure rather than lovers of God, holding to a form of godliness, although they have denied its power" (2 Tim. 3:2-5).

We should not only be concerned for those who are left to pick up the pieces of their shattered lives, but we should also listen to the many who are sworn to preserve life in our society. A host of doctors have raised a chorus of concern and condemnation regarding MMA and boxing. How much should be sacrificed to satisfy people's blood-lust? With our increased technological advances in medicine, we have a greater and growing awareness of the effects and consequences of violence in sport on those who practice these brutal arts. Is their concern regarding the sacrifice of human lives justified?

BLOOD SACRIFICE

Perhaps one of the most easily missed, yet important, reasons why gladiatorial contests were initiated was that they were seen as human blood sacrifices. "Tomb frescoes from Paestum (350 BC) show paired-fighters in a propitiatory funeral blood-rite that anticipates early Roman gladiator games."[153] In their earliest form, gladiatorial contests were known to involve slaves who would fight at someone's funeral. This was not done purely for the sake of entertainment; it was performed in honor of the dead. A human blood sacrifice was, in fact, made to appease their spirits. "Gladiatorial games (*munera*) originated in the rites of sacrifice due the spirits of the dead and the need to propitiate them with offerings of blood."[154]

The Romans also expanded this to incorporate these spectacles into the celebrations after a victory. Again, one of the main reasons was to propitiate (satisfy) the gods so that they would send blessings. In the formal Roman gladiatorial games, the obvious religious overtones are often unrecognized by moderns. "The religious component in gladiatorial ceremonies continued to be important. For example, attendants in the arena were dressed up as gods."[155]

In our day, human blood sacrifice is not always obvious to us because we don't usually think in these terms, but the link is very real. The Roman crowds enjoyed god-like powers in the arena, choosing if a fallen gladiator would live or die. Abortion, at its very core, is a human blood sacrifice acceptable within our culture. Myriads of children are daily sacrificed to the god of self and choice. The joys and aspirations of one person, or the collective society, is at the expense of someone's life, and globally, hundreds of millions of unborn babies have paid the price.

Another form of blood sacrifice within popular culture can be found in horror movies and other genres of film. These depictions are an attempt to satisfy the lust for blood, offering various forms of human sacrifice. When we look at human blood sacrifice, it comes in many forms. Boxers have been sacrificed (murdered) before cheering crowds. Long-term health issues such as brain damage and early death are the sacrifices made for short-term glory and gratification. Family units have been sacrificed as children are left fatherless for the love of money. Divorce, due to depression, and anger have emerged. How much is Western society ready to sacrifice to quench its thirst?

MMA, THE MOST DANGEROUS "SPORT"?

"However, it's hard not to be squeamish at the amount of blood some fights have . . . or when a fighter is knocked out by a quick strike to the head and falls like a rag doll."[156] The danger for us as researchers and readers alike is that many names and numbers can begin to numb our minds to reality. People can become nameless statistics, which can actually blind us to the fact that we are dealing with human life. We must remember that many cases involve an individual being rushed to the hospital with blood pooling in the brain.

Medical staff see what we hope we never will. Brain hemorrhaging, bruising, grotesque swelling, screams, and the silence of death. We can attempt to sanitize our world to cope, but the bloodied consequences remain. The horrible reality we may catch through a news article cannot be truly overstated. We all run the risk at this point of allowing our love for each individual person to become cold. Jesus warns that, "Because lawlessness is increased, most people's love will grow cold" (Matt. 24:12). We who name the name of Christ do not have this option. Where we fail, God does not; each person created in the image of God gains His unwavering attention.

Pertaining to injuries, it is only prudent to turn to the medical community to hear what it has to say. One would think that its voice would be heard and adhered to in such matters. But ironically, it is clearly being ignored. More research and more long-term studies are called for as the mounting death toll rises. In 2008, the British Medical Association, along with eleven other associations—including Canada, Australia, New Zealand, and South Africa—called for an outright ban on boxing and MMA.[157]

Even the World Medical Association (WMA) is quoted as stating, "Boxing is a dangerous sport. Unlike most other sports, its basic intent is to produce bodily harm in the opponent . . . For this reason, the World Medical Association recommends that boxing be banned."[158] The WMA additionally called for a full ban on MMA at its 2017 General Assembly held in Chicago.[159]

The British Medical Association also makes no distinction between boxing and Mixed Martial Arts. "As with boxing the BMA opposes mixed martial arts (MMA) fighting and calls for a complete ban on this type of contact sport."[160] Apparently, amongst much of the medical community, there need not be any quibbling about which of these two sports is safer.

It should disturb us that those who have taken an oath to preserve life and those who would come with great authority on health issues are intentionally disregarded. One begins to get the impression that the truth is plain to see, but society is becoming increasingly blinded. The debate about which is more dangerous is a moot point from a medical standpoint; yet the data—as one would expect—is starting to reveal the truth. One such example is, "Acute and long term injuries are prevalent—unsurprising considering that the force of a professional boxer's punch is comparable with being hit with a 6 kg bowling ball traveling at 32 km/hour."[161]

More regulation, more studies, and safer rules continue to be heralded by those in support of boxing and MMA. Boxers argue that MMA is only in its infancy, and a fair comparison can't be made; while MMA argues that in contrast, more boxers have died. Ultimately, all studies affirm the intent to inflict bodily harm and the brutal results.

One study in the *American Journal of Sports Medicine* in 2014 found that MMA fighters suffer traumatic brain injury in almost a third of professional bouts. "The rate is far more than the occurrence of such injuries in hockey, football or even boxing."[162] The study examined seven years of fights, which recorded a knockout or technical knockout ending the fight.

They also visually reviewed the fights and saw that the most startling revelation was the repeated blows to the head after the fighter had been knocked unconscious. The fighter is completely defenseless to such blows. There is no ten-count for a downed opponent as in boxing. Not only this, but UFC formerly had a bonus for the "knockout of the night." This bonus ceased in 2014, but the brain damage has not.

Medically speaking, each concussion by knockout produces brain damage. It is unbelievable that concussions are of such concern; yet, in the UFC (prior to 2014), you were given "knockout of the night" bonuses to concuss your opponent. From another study eight years earlier, a 2006 paper published in the *Journal of Sports Science and Medicine* concluded that "the overall injury rate in MMA competitions is now similar to other combat sports including boxing. Knockout rates are lower in MMA competitions than in boxing."[163]

Despite these factors, the legendary boxer Sugar Ray Robinson summed up the issue when he resentfully shot back at a lawyer who questioned him as to why he did not restrain himself after seeing his opponent so injured. Sugar Ray killed his rival, Jimmy Doyle, with his own hands. His response was, "Sir, it is my business to hurt people."[164]

MMA supporters continually cite the violent nature of tackle football as a reason for justifying their combat sport. If the octagon is wrong, why not the gridiron? There are obvious differences between the two; one wears protective equipment to eliminate or lesson injury, while the goal of the other, by its nature, is to inflict bodily harm.

Secondly, similar to hockey, fighting is actually illegal in the game of football. Especially in football, serious penalties are given for offending players. The *true nature* of football and hockey do not exclude them from being named legitimate sports. The *British Medical Journal* states, "Boxing (and by extension MMA), therefore, cannot be justified on health and safety grounds as an appropriate or legitimate 'sport.'"[165]

A further distinction can be made between football and other sports. It was reported in contrast to football, that "during the 2013-14 academic year, no other high school sport directly killed even one athlete."[166] On these grounds, MMA and boxing supporters have a point. Contact football, though not a blood sport, is an attack on an individual that has caused catastrophic effects. I believe Christians should be the ones to raise the alarm and not be supportive of any sports that intentionally attack the image of God.

Surprisingly, the most dangerous sport, statistically, is cheerleading. Throwing young ladies high into the air to be caught only by human hands is truly an act of faith. Similar to other sports, there have been great attempts to limit catastrophic injury on various levels. "College teams are no longer allowed to perform three-person-high pyramids and do double flips from them. High school teams can't perform flipping basket tosses and last year, twisting dismounts were banned on basketball courts."[167]

Cheerleading ought to be made safe. Furthermore, cheerleading shows that there are obvious differences between what is dangerous and what is violence. The question remains: Can humanity apart from God even come up with a sound definition for violence? The truth is, what humanity clouds, the Scripture makes clear.

WHAT IS VIOLENCE?

The writer to the Hebrews makes it very clear that discerning good and evil is not always easy, yet also not impossible. "But solid food is for the mature, who because of practice have their senses trained to discern good and evil" (Heb. 5:14). When it comes to the issue of defining violence, it might not be as easy as one thinks. Violence, according to the World Health Organization, is "the intentional use of physical force or power, threatened or actual, against oneself, another person, or against a group or community, which either results in or has a high likelihood of resulting in injury, death, psychological harm, maldevelopment, or deprivation."[168] Violence includes the idea of intentionally hurting another person. Boxing and MMA blatantly fall into this category.

Yet, the WHO definition could be challenged in relation to civil order if not carefully qualified. If a gunman or terrorist has a firearm directed at someone's head in a hostage situation and a police sniper kills him, was this an act of violence? Injury and death are the result, and an attempt to harm was present. But does it fit within the broad scope of what is generally called violence?

Much attention, in recent years, has been given to what is called "police violence." Police violence is seen as having occurred when an action has gone beyond reasonable force. If this were not true, any force by a police officer could be deemed violence. One begins to understand the nature of violence in its relationship to a word closely related to its root meaning to "violate."

The Latin word *violātus* appears linguistically to be derived from the word *violentus*, which is where we get our word violence.[169] A violation is related to that which breaks or transgresses a law. If a police sniper kills a terrorist who is transgressing the law, the officer himself is not the lawbreaker. Scripture says in reference to the ruling authorities, "For it is a minister of God to you for good. But if you do what is evil, be afraid; for it does not bear the sword for nothing; for it is a minister of God, an avenger who brings wrath on the one who practices evil" (Rom. 13:4).

Abortion is violence against unborn babies because it is a violation of God's law against a human being created in His image. Yet many governments and police forces will support doctors who commit these crimes. This act of violence has been redefined as compassion toward and free choice for women. This is where God's law supersedes man's laws. This is where God's actions to mete out justice supersedes any human action. Is it wrong for a man to kill an abortionist? Absolutely, because the killer has violated God's law. The Bible says, "Never pay back evil for evil to anyone . . . 'VENGEANCE IS MINE, I WILL REPAY,' says the Lord" (Rom. 12:17, 19).

To gain a true definition of violence against humans, it must always find its way back to God's Law and His first principles. Violence is the intentional infliction of harm; it occurs when it violates one created in God's image, thereby violating God's law.

HOW SHOULD BELIEVERS RESPOND?

Concussions can happen in everyday life by just slipping on the floor. They can happen even in physical activity and sport with the most innocent intent.

The issue becomes thorny when violence is accepted. A number of articles have appeared seeking to address the issue for believers, where violence is inherent in a sport.

Christianity's Concussion Crisis: Where Football and Faith Collide talks about the embracing of football by many who "have often uncritically used the sport as a vehicle for their religious messages . . . It was as if the caretakers of American football had made a contract with the propagators of American religion, agreeing that football would serve religion, but only if it was granted immunity for the ways it could damage bodies young and old."[170] A *USA Today* author in "NFL Violence a Moral Thorn for Christians" states, "For this respecter of faith and morality it's no longer possible to enjoy watching the game. The agenda for fall Sundays and Monday nights has changed, and football ain't on it."[171]

When it comes to being followers of Christ in relation to sport, the apostle Paul speaks of himself as boxing and combating his own body into submission, not someone else's (1 Cor. 9:26-27). Paul never wanted believers to turn their fists for sport on others, but to use the weapons of prayer and Scripture.

The fact is that any sporting activity which seeks to attack an individual created in the image of God should not be engaged in nor endorsed. Beyond football, boxing and MMA are clearly blood sports. The sole purpose of these "sports" is to hurt and render immobile an individual. The blood-lust is so very clear. People can try to sanctify and justify it by calling it a "sport," but the blood-bought Christian should be encouraged to walk a better path and even stand opposed to such activities. Prayer brought victory for the early church, and believers need to continue this pattern in praying for and loving all involved.

Author Gary Wills states in his article, "Blood Lust and the Super Bowl," "After I met brain-damaged Muhammad Ali, I vowed never to watch another boxing event, and never have. Perhaps, if violence is the essence of football, I should give that up too."[172] Violence has infiltrated games such as football and hockey. Many people are now just becoming aware of this pro-life issue, since the human collateral damage is so high. It is not easy to go against the tide, yet Scripture affirms that there is a better road to travel than following the crowd.

CHAPTER 6

THE NEW ROME ARISING?

"Those who cannot remember the past are condemned to repeat it."

—George Santayana[173]

MARCH 22, 2016, IS PERHAPS an obscure date in the annals of history, yet it marked a silent but monumental day in the arena of Mixed Martial Arts. New York finally lifted its twenty-year ban on MMA.[174] The final state holdout, being a bit out of touch with the rest of the forty-nine states, finally succumbed to the inevitable. The fight to legalize MMA was finally won with little more than a whimper. The clutch of this sport has predictably enveloped the whole of the United States. It is an undeniable fact that what happens in the USA reverberates around the world. Yet this is a movement that has less to do with the USA, but more to do with the violent chronicles of human history rushing headlong toward a moral meltdown. Some may see this claim as a "tempest in a tea pot," but the culminating evidence speaks otherwise.

April 9, 2016—perhaps another obscure date in the annals of history—marked a silent but deadly day for João Carvalho. Portugal's Carvalho took numerous blows to the nose in the third round of his MMA fight in Dublin, Ireland's National Boxing Stadium.[175] Twenty minutes after his fight, he began to vomit and was rushed to the hospital. Two days later, he died. Regulation would again be heralded as an answer. Yet extreme fighting had again snuffed out the life of another young man, almost three weeks after its total acceptance in the USA. The currents of human history continue to move forward in a powerful and somewhat predictable fashion.

"It is, admittedly, an American-centric point of view, that this sport founded in the US and spreading throughout the world ought to ascend to the Olympics in a flash . . . Later this year comes an event in England and the first UFC event in China, the world's most populous country. The case is already being made on a worldwide level that mixed martial arts could be an Olympic sport as early as 2020."[176]

Whether or not MMA will ascend to the Olympics is yet to be seen, but the momentum of human trends is moving strongly toward the day when it will once again take the podium. It has been the intention of this book to chronicle the history of gladiators with its long history and fall in the West. In time, Christianity's persecuted beginnings intersected with ancient gladiators. The eventual outcome was the defeat of this blood sport.

The resurrection of blood sports in the West led to a clash with the influences of Christianity and one of its first principles as humans being created in the image of God. Now, with the increasing decline of Christian influence in Western society, its almost predictable trajectory is ascending, historically speaking, "in a flash." Will this momentum take gladiators to its fullest extent within a new Rome?

As the world rushes forward, I do not purport to know exactly how events will unfold, other than what Scripture clearly tells us. Yet the Bible declares the extent of the sinful human nature and gives clues as to how this world will be in the end. Jesus said that a time of tribulation will come beyond anything ever experienced, and "Unless the Lord had shortened *those* days, no life would have been saved" (Mark 13:20).

It is no secret that the book of Revelation talks of global destruction. Scripture gives us markers as world history unfolds in an often-bizarre but somewhat predictable trajectory. During this journey together, I have sought to lay out many indicators of where we are within the scope of

Western civilization. With abortion, euthanasia, and violent entertainment gripping the West, a call to return to God's standard, with respect to all those who are vulnerable in our society, must once again grip us. Vice President Hubert Humphrey rightly stated, "The moral test of government is how the government treats those who are in the dawn of life, the children; those who are in the twilight of life, the elderly; those who are in the shadows of life; the sick, the needy and the handicapped."[177]

Are there any other indicators that we are losing our moral compass in the West?

Avalanche looked out of the big glass window of the gym as she pounded away on the treadmill. The rain was coming down in sheets, lashing against the window while the wind howled through the cracks. Her legs and lungs burned painfully as she glanced down at the treadmill's odometer to see how many miles she had run. Her big night in the cage was fast approaching. She swallowed back a twinge of fear that rippled through her, but quickly shrugged it aside, determined that once again her grit would see her through.

Her six-days-a-week training schedule was grueling, working tirelessly at practicing her punches and kicks. Although she hadn't yet sustained a serious injury in the cage, Avalanche knew it was always a possibility. After five long years of training, she was finally gaining confidence in her abilities. She knew, however, that her takedowns were her weakest point. That resulted in her coach spending many additional hours with her going over footage of previous fights so that she could recognize specific areas in which she might improve.

Avalanche also knew that she would have to lose four pounds in the next two days to "make weight."[178] If not, she would be disqualified. This was not an easy prospect, but it had to be done. As an up-and-coming star, she would soon be facing stiffer and stiffer competition. Perhaps after a few more fights, she might even be able to challenge the titleholder, Venom.

Hitting the treadmill's stop button, she stepped off the apparatus and quickly went through a series of uppercuts, finishing with a hard right hook.

Called a "tiny gladiator," Avalanche is ten years old.

"TINY GLADIATORS"

Many who support the issue of violence in sport argue that people *choose* to play these sports; so, it is a matter of freedom of choice. This idea sounds good, but it is flawed. We all make choices, yet not all choices should we be free to make. Someone might choose to rob another person at gunpoint, but we would all agree that they are not free to do so. For lines of truth to be drawn, they must come from the source of all truth, no matter how inconvenient or seemingly unprofitable they may appear.

One would hope that when it comes to tender children, "civilized" societies would draw a line. But the line has also faded. Children should not be endorsed or encouraged to be in the business of hurting one another. If we can't see this, our society is in big trouble. The Bible warns that after repeated rejections of God, which we know has happened in Western civilization, the end result is to be given over to a mind that is unapproved by God. Romans 1:28, states, "And just as they did not see fit to acknowledge God any longer, God gave them over to a depraved mind, to do those things which are not proper."

The moral decline in the West is no secret. A Gallup poll shows that "more than four in five (81%) now rate the state of moral values in the U.S. as only fair or poor." And "77% say the state of moral values is getting worse."[179] The indictments against the West's decline continues to stack higher. The concerns are highlighted in *Huffington Post*'s investigative report titled "Exploring the Dark World of Children's MMA."[180]

It has been documented on *ABC News* that children as young as five years old are fighting.[181] The thought of it seems to be so repulsive, but it is true. One of the most disturbing parts of the news report is two little five-year-old girls striking each other before cheering onlookers. Child Pankration is supposed to be different than MMA because it doesn't allow strikes to the head. But as it has been well-documented, many children still suffer the pain of getting struck in the face.

Andy Foster, a former MMA fighter himself and executive of the California State Athletic Commission, was shocked and "started shutting down MMA youth events in May of 2013 after seeing a video of a 5-year-old girl being pummeled by a larger boy."[182] He feels he has been forced to regulate the youth events and says, "I don't think we can get rid of it even if I wanted."[183] "In a 2008 article, MMA commentator Sam Caplan wrote that 'It should be illegal for anyone under the age of 18 to compete in a mixed martial arts fight.'"[184]

Many doctors again are clearly concerned about the effects that this type of activity has on young children. Their bones are not yet fully developed, and the damage that can be done is physically and emotionally unknown. Yet common sense and experience should affirm what science will only confirm. *ABC News* reported on one child female fighter who suffered defeat at the hands of her rival and sobbed uncontrollably.

The effects of emotional trauma cannot be underestimated. Former UFC women's champion Ronda Rousey says she was so grief-stricken by her loss to Holly Holm that she seriously considered suicide.[185] Sadly, Holly Holm's fight name is "The Preacher's Daughter." Her father is a pastor, who has supported her endeavors.

All the anti-bullying campaigns have a somewhat hollow ring in a society that would tolerate children fighting one another for show. Should we endorse the sacrificing of childhood at the altar of MMA? The Pankration children of today will be the MMA fighters of tomorrow. By having endorsed Mixed Martial Arts yesterday, we opened the door for child Pankration today.

How did Dana White, President of Ultimate Fighting Championship, respond when questioned about child cage fighting? In an interview on *CBS's* morning show regarding children fighting in cages, Dana quips in a sales pitch, "It's fun and it's safe."[186] The World Medical Association itself states that no child should be allowed to participate in such a combat sport.[187] A flashback in history would reveal that within the ancient Roman Empire, children, before they hit puberty, were being trained for gladiatorial combat.[188]

"WE ARE DEFINITELY IN ROME."[189]

—Dr. Albert Mohler Jr.,
President of Southern Baptist Theological Seminary

> Then there will be a fourth kingdom as strong as iron; inasmuch as iron crushes and shatters all things, so, like iron that breaks into pieces, it will crush and break all these in pieces. In that you saw the feet and toes, partly of potter's clay and partly of iron, it will be a divided kingdom; but it will have in it the toughness of iron, inasmuch as you saw the iron mixed with common clay (Dan. 2:40-41).

Within the ancient writings of the biblical book of Daniel is contained a prophesy and a panoramic picture of future world history. This was revealed in a dream to King Nebuchadnezzar of Babylon. Daniel was given the interpretation of the dream by God, and he was able to explain, without prior knowledge, not only what the king saw but also what it meant. How often have Sunday school teachers rightly taught the statue of Daniel to children, and yet it speaks profoundly to all of us?

The king's dream consisted of a statue that had a head of gold representing mighty Babylon. It also had a breast and arms of silver representing the daunting Medo-Persian Empire. The belly and thighs of bronze speak of the vast, influential Greek Empire led, most notably, by Alexander the Great. The legs were of iron and the feet of iron and clay, declaring the fourth kingdom as the crushing, mighty Roman Empire. The beauty of Daniel's prophesy is that this oft-quoted Sunday school story is historically true. The great empires that have risen and fallen and whose influence has been incorporated into the others stand as testimony to the truth of God's predictive Word.

With this in mind, we should move on with great care and consideration about what the Bible says will come. Very often, End Times discussions are surrounded by what divides believers. Yet the legs representing the mighty Roman Empire extending into the feet mixed with iron and clay has been the overwhelmingly dominant view held by Christians, Jews, and Bible scholars for over two thousand years.[190] [191]

Another dominant view amongst Christians and Jews is that the Stone, which finally crushes all the kingdoms, is a reference to the Messiah and His kingdom (Dan. 2:35).[192] At Christ's future return, it is He—the Stone (Matt. 21:42-43)—Who hits the feet and crushes the entire statue, leaving no trace. The feet which He hits still possesses iron, an extension of the Roman Empire. We need not press the imagery so far that we cannot see a future aspect of Rome, for even Babylon (a prior empire) is mentioned in Revelation.

Though varied groups and views about the End Times have emerged, the identity of the first four empires is not usually in question. It follows that if the fourth empire is Rome, then the iron part of the feet points us toward a re-vitalized Roman Empire. The Bible says that a final phase of this empire will appear which has both a toughness of iron (represented as Rome) and the brittleness of clay. It is a divided kingdom. Many term it as the neo (new) or revived Roman Empire, which is the dominant of the two substances, the clay being the weaker factor. Only the Kingdom of the Messiah will bring the mixture to a crushing end.

One interesting indication of the New Roman Empire emerging is the area of globalization and the uniting of nations. The statue with the golden head, Babylon, takes our minds back to the tower of Babel, where there used to be one unified language and people (Gen. 11:1-9). In judgment, God separated the peoples of the world by the confusion of languages. Today, people possessing thousands of languages and dialects are now being connected by one Western language. For the first time since Babel, one global language has now emerged, namely English, in the global village we call home.

It is extremely common for many teachers from differing views to agree that we are nearing the Lord's return. We don't know the exact time or day, but as Paul says, "But you, brethren, are not in darkness, that the day would overtake you like a thief" (1 Thess. 5:4). There are many indications in Scripture for Christians that Christ's return should not be a complete surprise, as it will be for the unbeliever. We do not know the day or the hour, but the seasons are and will increasingly become evident.

I find it both striking and compelling to see that at the very time the West is in moral decay and Christianity's influence continues to decline, the social attraction so much at the heart of ancient Roman society is being resurrected. Are there any other clues to the resurrection of a New Roman Empire?

TECHNOLOGICAL TWIST

> *"What are we Ancient Rome here? Is it going to be, like,*
> *lions in the ring next?"*
> —Former Fox News Host Bill O'Reilly to
> UFC President Dana White[193]

The fascination with ancient combat sports has not stopped with boxing and hand-to-hand Mixed Martial Arts. In the article titled, "Company Wants to Resurrect Gladiators—With a Modern Twist," we are introduced to an Australian company called Unified Weapons Master (UWM).[194] The lure of gladiatorial combat is realized from another direction. Another article, entitled "Unified Weapons Master Brings Us Back to the Colosseum," states, "Well, mankind might have advanced to be a whole lot more civilized these days, but there is still the primal call of blood-lust. Having said that, we can now engage in full contact weapons fighting without spilling a single drop of blood."[195]

The UWM combat took place within a ring, which sported two armed warriors wielding various ancient weapons. Each combatant was suited with carbon fiber armor that was filled with sensors. As the battle ensued, each hit was measured by a computer with data parameters. The commentator took the viewer through the action, and computer data was continually updating each fighter's standings. Every strike was calculated in real time to render the data according to how much force it would take to literally break a bone, inflict a wound, or give a death blow if it were performed without protection. The strikes lead the fight to its intended end: *virtual death.*

The glamor of martial arts and weaponry was packaged in something like a video game, but with real humans fighting. Unified Weapons Master (UWM) attempted to set the stage to storm the world of combat sport. Members were called Gladiators. CEO David Pysden said, "There is nowhere in the world you can go right now and watch two people fighting with samurai swords, and we're going to change that."[196]

After its debut fight on social media, more than one million hits were documented. That was a significant amount of interest generated for its inauguration. UWM appears to have failed in making any further inroads, but it is telling how the lure of the ancient gladiatorial games in Rome captured significant interest.

BATTLE OF THE NATIONS

The lure of the arena now includes the resurrection of weaponry in a more realistic and dangerous venue, which some have termed "Medieval MMA."[197] One such event that draws thousands of fans each year is the Historical Medieval Battles (HMB) staged in Europe.

"HMB is a new sport that combines a modern approach to the organization of sporting events and ancient martial arts. It's a new stage of martial arts development, based on the techniques of the Middle Ages and the latest achievements of modern full contact sports."[198] Starting with just four teams in 2009, "Battle of the Nations" has even grown to see the representatives of thirty countries battling it out in a fenced ring.

Teams from the USA, Russia, Canada, Britain, Australia, and a host of other nations engage in a barrage of full contact battles behind metal armaments using traditional weapons such as blunted swords and axes. "Battle of the Nations" is full contact fighting using forged metal weapons from the Middle Ages. Fighters dress in armor, which is also made according to historical standards.[199] Combat includes one-on-one, five-on-five, and mass battles of twenty-one individuals per team who engage in an absolute full-throttle brawl. The armor appears impressive, but the blunt force and brutality of such battles can only provide so much protection. The humanness behind the armor can easily be lost—and the fact that these people are created in the image of God. Bloody noses, concussions, and broken bones are not unknown in such engagements.

These festive events are held at ancient castle sites and various locations in Europe, which no doubt lend themselves to the allure of these engagements. The revelry of drinking and merrymaking is also a part of the whole production as medieval times and flavors fill the air. Music, costumes, food, and fans are all a part of the outdoor festivities, which happens once per year. All of the excitement can cloud the insidious appeal to a generation being lured to ever-greater heights of combat sports.

The recent ratcheting up of fights using actual weapons further supports the view that something of global significance is going on here. The historical landscape we have observed and the almost predictable trajectory is being further entrenched as this new brand of combat sport continues to grow in acceptance and popularity around the world. We continue to ask, just how popular will this new, destructive form of sport become, and how far will the combatants go to win the approval of their fans?

We have now taken another step closer and are truly only one step away from the full return of gladiators. It is startling to realize that it would only take the removal of certain pieces of armor, and we will have full-fledged gladiatorial fights once again. How far this will go, only the Lord truly knows.

COULD IT RETURN?

When we think of the countless lives that have been saved over the centuries by the most enduring influence of early Christianity in ending gladiatorial combat, we can rejoice in God's goodness. Yet should we be comforted by the idea that a number of scholars are unable to fathom its return? One scholar states, "It is hard for the modern reader not to be alienated by the idea that the sight of a man struggling against the pain of a fatal wound can constitute a source of edification and visual joy."[200] Fagan would counter this statement by saying, "The annually increasing scale of death and destruction in summer blockbuster movies rather suggests otherwise."[201]

To catch a glimpse of how people are thinking, social media does have its place in research. One blogger on an internet forum posed a question which garnered many responses: "If it was allowed, would an arena with gladiators fighting to the death prove popular in modern times?" The majority of respondents (two-thirds) affirmed that it would.[202] Matthew Naismith of Australia, the originator of the question, also gave his own answer: "I think it would be packed out myself which just shows how bad our intellectual and moral selves have deteriorated back to sensationalism of the good old days of the Roman Empire which has many similarities to the present empire we are living under today, what do you think?"[203] Gale Kooser also stated, "We may cloak ourselves with intellect and morals, but that cloak is tissue thin. So yes! Those arenas would be full and the protesters would be outside."[204]

Could humans justify such cruelty again as they did in the Roman Empire? Is there anything redemptive about gladiatorial games? Some may argue yes. The Romans allowed a criminal to redeem himself through fighting in the gladiatorial ring. After many victories, a gladiator could receive the prized wooden sword and be set free into retirement.

One can see the "humane" and humanistic logic behind the Roman's sense of morality and mercy. This reasoning, though deeply flawed, gives us an idea of how the Romans could feel justified as offering "redemption" to those in the ring, in the midst of such evil. Arguments like this, containing a little moral twist, could be the basis for justifying its return in the future.

Paralleling this, Fagan, author of the book *The Lure of the Arena*, has some sobering words for us.

> The distance between the Roman gladiator arena and the modern American football stadium is not as far as we might think or wish . . . I suspect if we staged a gladiator spectacle and we picked the right constituency to staff it—people who are commonly regarded by society as expendable, such as death row inmates—I think we could fill Beaver Stadium.[205]

> Fagan suggests that the desire for violent entertainment appears not just in the arena—and not just in Ancient Rome or America . . . "Looking across the landscape of history we have to admit there's something bigger going on, a consistent appetite for violence as spectacle." The recent rise of the Ultimate Fighting Championship, a mixed martial arts sport noted for its brutality, strikes Fagan as a prime example.[206]

The Bible says that the mystery of evil is actually being held back, but one day its full-blown potential will be realized. "For the mystery of lawlessness is already at work; only he who now restrains *will do so* until he is taken out of the way" (2 Thess. 2:7). The gladiatorial attraction is real and profound in our world today and should not be underestimated.

Professor Kathleen Coleman of Harvard reminds us that with all the glamor and pomp, the gladiatorial games were extremely addictive.[207] Professor David Potter adds that the lure of the arena was the "feeling of a suddenly created society and a common interest."[208] Though it can seem unfathomable that sanctioned gladiatorial fights to the death could happen again, my own experience continues to reinforce my concern.

In my personal research, I have had the opportunity to talk with a number of young men, and the present lure of the arena has become very obvious to me. I have been amazed at how many will actually admit that if fighting to the death became legal, they would or might go to watch it under certain conditions (i.e. not with slaves, but with voluntary fighters). Though a strong segment have expressed that they would not, the reality of what is going on in human hearts is very revealing.

We, who are believers, should be aware that the addictive nature of combat and blood sports will only call for more. We should stand up, speak up, and be counted, so that we also can be involved in saving physically and spiritually the lives of those who are heading toward potential physical and spiritual destruction.

THE CALL

> "And I heard another voice from heaven, saying: 'Come out of her, my people, so that you may not have fellowship in her sins, and so that you may not receive of her plagues' . . . And in her was found *the* blood of prophets and of saints and of all those having been slain on the earth" (Rev. 18:4, 24 BLB).

When we see Heaven calling us as believers to be separate from the emerging world order to come, the call to "come out" is clear. We have a great responsibility to resist all the seductive ways of the world and to proclaim Christ's victory and coming kingdom. Jesus foretold that in the end, the similarities between the world to come and the world from which Noah escaped are stark. Jesus focused on the more relaxed, *indifferent and indulgent* way of life. Yet He knew very well what the other defining features of the world that perished in Noah's day were. The world was completely corrupt and filled with violence (Gen. 6:11, 13).

In contrast to the ease of this life, Jesus said, "For what does it profit a man to gain the whole world, and forfeit his soul" (Mark 8:36). The text implies that the worth of one individual created in God's image is valued more than the entire world. If the love of Jesus was so great and His blood so precious to deliver even one sinner, how momentous is His work in allowing His blood to be shed for the sins of the whole world (1 John 2:2). He is the ultimate example of separation from an indifferent, indulgent, corrupt, and violent world; He is the One Whom we must emulate.

> "And I saw the woman being drunk with the blood of the saints, and with the blood of the witnesses of Jesus" (Rev. 17:6 BLB).

When we look back in history, it was the Christians who would not bow to the Roman emperor as their lord. As we discuss things difficult to fathom, we need the same eye of faith that they had to stand against Imperial Rome, believing they would ultimately be victorious. How easy it would have been to conform, yet these were the ones who allowed themselves to be drenched with their own blood. They were amongst those who would be included as sideshows to the gladiators and other events. The blood of the saints was spilled in this alluring forum. Yet, amazingly, they were the victors!

Do those of us who remain on the Earth today, with the emerging trends, think that somehow we could never experience persecution like that again? Can we embrace and walk a path that in time could cause the blood of saints to flow? The world of the future will not only be "drunk" with blood, but with the blood of true believers. This is not being alarmist, but a realist, for Scripture speaks of "the woman being drunk with the blood of the saints." We need to be willing and prepared, by God's grace, to suffer as the early believers did, for the sake of righteousness (Act 5:41).

John Oswalt, in his Isaiah commentary, has some extremely insightful conclusions: "Idolatry is the manifestation of the human thirst for glory . . . 'Modern Humanism is simply ancient idolatry in a three-piece suit or a pair of designer jeans' . . . But the marvel of humanity is our capacity to resurrect the old pride from the ruins and refurbish it again."[209]

The apostle Paul states that we are to "put no confidence in the flesh" (Phil. 3:3). It is easy to think such activities will not affect us nor infect the world to such extremes. With these ideas, could not our confidence be misplaced? As the author, I hope it never happens, but I hold no confidence in humanity's ability to stop itself from eventually returning to full-fledged gladiators. Even scholars in various mediums have warned us to be careful not to assume it couldn't happen again. The words of Professor Andrew Wallace are worth repeating, "Could we be like it or are they completely different from us?—and I think we know that there is a bit in us that is absolutely there with the Romans. We could be like them."[210]

Scripture says Christ will build His Church, and the gates of Hades will not prevail against it; yet, humanity will continue to seek to build its own congregants and kingdom as well. The blood-bought should be encouraged to stand (as did our brothers and sisters in ancient Rome) against blood sports, *for without Christ, humanity is set to do it again.*

AFTERWORD

"LOCKDOWN"—THIS NOW PREVALENT WORD TOOK on a whole new meaning as I looked into the concerned faces of my students in Wuhan. It seemed inconceivable to me that eleven million people in one city were locked within their apartments. The Covid cases were rising exponentially in the city from one week to the next. Teaching English online to Chinese students allowed me to get an extremely early knowledge that something earth-shattering had just silently erupted. The distant reverberations could hardly be explained to others for whom Wuhan was unknown.

Since then, the world has seen governments scramble to contain the silent explosion. Differing views and opinions do not change the fact that the world has changed. It has sent us spiraling with mind-bending speed toward what the Bible has predicted for thousands of years. What caught my attention was the rumblings within the news media to blame Christians for the crisis. This sounded reminiscent of the Roman Empire.

This book was penned before the Coronavirus crisis, and the guidebook of Scripture allowed us, on some level, to expect what we see even today. The teachings of Scripture against racism, flagrantly ignored through pride and Darwinian evolutionism, erupted into global significance with the tragic and horrible death of George Floyd. One act led to retaliations that sent streets ablaze and caused chaos to ensue. Race reconciliation is a worldly attempt to do what God shows is terribly misguided. As pointed out in this book, there is only *one race*. This highlights the absolute importance of grasping the significance and truth that we all, no matter our skin color, are created in God's image. We are to love our neighbors as ourselves.

The Bible also warns us of increasing lawlessness, deception, violence, and a decrease in human love toward others. Calls to literally abolish police forces were heralded as a step forward as city fires raged. Previously, the world appeared unstoppable with its economic highs and prosperity, and yet the economic desolations and collapses Scripture discusses can now begin to be understood in real time.

We recognize that as the world governments synchronize their responses, pressure to conform on all levels will increase. Again, no matter what views are held, there is no doubt that the theme of a one-world government, fashioned by the elite, rumbles toward the rise of an empire like the Rome of old. This empire will become increasingly hostile to the Church and the people of God. This is a pivotal time in world history for God's people to remember the past, understand the present, and prepare for the future.

ENDNOTES

CHAPTER 1

1. This is a fictional story based on historical realities.

2. G.G. Fagan, *The Lure of the Arena: Social Psychology and the Crowd at the Roman Games* (Cambridge: Cambridge University Press, 2011), 286.

3. T.J. Simers, "The Life of a UFC Wife: The Modern Gladiators Do Battle, You Feel the Pain." *The New Ledger: Los Angeles Times*, July 2009.

4. Russel Hoye et al., *Sport Management: Principles and Application* (New York: Routledge 2015), 12:3.

5. Kristen Peterson, "The Art in UFC's Violence," *Las Vegas Sun*, http://www.lasvegassun.com/news/2008/may/22/ art-ufcs-violence, accessed April 20, 2016.

6. Fagan, 271.

7. *Gladiators: Back From the Dead,* Directed by Jeremy Turner, 2010, Channel 4, TV Documentary. London, England, June 14, 2010. The exceptionally longer arm, as compared with the other, from the skeleton of a gladiator shows the signs of intensive training before the age of puberty. This is commonly recognized in sports medicine. Young children who are trained intensively in tennis, with the constant repetition of hitting the ball, will show similar signs.

8. A. Futrell, *The Roman Games* (Malden, MA: Blackwell Publishing, 2006), 62.

9. Merriam-Webster Dictionary, s.v. "gladiator," http://www.merriam-webster.com/dictionary/gladiator, accessed June 12, 2011.

10. T. Wiedemann, *Emperors and Gladiators* (London and New York: Routledge, 1992), 94.

11. L. Jacobelli, *Gladiators at Pompeii* (Los Angeles: Getty Publications, 2003), 39.

12. Wiedemann, 57.

13. Fagan, 237.

14. Futrell, 146.

15. *Gladiator Games: The Roman Bloodsport*, Prod. John Pattyson, et. al (TV 2000 Documentary), November 21, 2000.

Pictures of the figurines can be found in *Gladiators at Pompeii* by Luciana Jacobelli, 101-102.

16. Fagan, 281.

17. Fagan, 214 n. 75.

18. Josh Brown, "Hominick Stole the Show at UFC 129," *The Record*, http://www.therecord.com/sports/local/article/531955—hominick-stole-the-show-at-ufc-129, accessed April 25, 2016.

19. Steve Buffery, "St. Pierre Stars but Hominick Steals the Show," *Toronto Sun*, http://www.torontosun.com/2011/05/01/st-pierre-stars-but-hominick-steals-the-show, accessed June 12, 2011.

20. Fagan, 272.

21. *Gladiators: Back From the Dead* (TV Documentary).

22. D. Deibert, "Brain Hemorrhage Forces Brian Foster off UFC 129 in Toronto," *Vancouver Sun*. Kicks to the groin are illegal in the UFC. There are thirty-one rules in the UFC.

23. Tertullian, "Spectacles," *Disciplinary, Moral and Ascetical Works* in *The Fathers of the Church,* trans. R. Arbesmann et al., vol. 40 (New York: Fathers of the Church, 1959), 93.

24. Fagan, *The Lure of the Arena,* 315.

25. Wiedemann, 102.

26. Fagan, 196 n. 23.

27. *Gladiator Games: The Roman Bloodsport,* (TV 2000 Documentary)

CHAPTER 2

28. This is a fictional story based on historical realities : Pliny's correspondence with Emperor Trajan (Letters 10:96, 10:97) and Tacitus's Annals (Book 15 Chap. 44).

29. H. Chadwick, *The Early Church* (New York: Penguin Books, 1967), 56.

30. Ibid, 26.

31. Ibid.

32. Paul R. Spickard et al., *A Global History of Christians: How Everyday Believers Experienced Their World* (Grand Rapids Michigan: Baker Academics, 1994), 44.

33. T. Wiedemann, *Emperors and Gladiators* (London and New York: Routledge, 1992), 146.

34. Ibid.

35. E. Rothstein, "Shelf Life; A Bioethicist's Take on Genesis," *The New York Times,* http://www.nytimes.com/2003/08/02/arts/02SHEL.html, accessed April 20, 2016.

36. Ibid.

37. Ibid.

38. Wiedemann, 130.

39. *Gladiator Games: Roman Blood Sport,* Exec. Prod.: John Pattyson, et. al (TV 2000 Documentary), November 21, 2000.

40. Ibid.

41. Augustine, *Confessions*, in Garry Wills, "Blood Lust and the Super Bowl," *The New York Review of Books*, http://www.nybooks.com/blogs/nyrblog/2011/feb/04/blood-lust-and-super-bowl, accessed April 27, 2016.

42. G.G. Fagan, *The Lure of the Arena: Social Psychology and the Crowd at the Roman Games* (Cambridge: Cambridge University Press, 2011), 279.

43. Merriam-Webster Dictionary, s.v. "vicariously," http://www.merriam-webster.com/dictionary/vicariously, accessed April 20, 2016.

44. A. Roberts and J. Donaldson, ed., "Theophilus of Antioch," *Ante-Nicene Fathers*, 2.223, in Ages Software, Oregon, 1997.

45. Wiedemann, 129-130.

46. Roberts and Donaldson ed., "Irenaus: Against Heresies," *Ante-Nicene Fathers*, 1. 1. 3. in Ages Software, Oregon, 1997, 641.

47. Roberts and Donaldson ed., "Address of Tatian to the Greeks," *Ante-Nicene Fathers*, 2.1., in Ages Software, Oregon, 1997, 138.

48. Roberts and Donaldson ed., "Latin Christianity: Its Founder, Tertullian," *Ante-Nicene Fathers*, 3.19., in Ages Software, Oregon, 1997, 160.

49. A. Curtis and J. Lang, *Dates with Destiny* (New York: Fleming H. Revel Company, 1991), 24.

50. Phillip Schaff and Henry Wace, *A Select Library of Nicene and Post-Nicene Fathers of the Christian Church*, Chapter 26, Vol. 3 (New York: The Christian Literature Company, 1892), 151.

51. "Boxing: An Ancient Tradition, A Necessary Skill," Boxing Herald.com. http://www.boxinghearld.com/boxing-news/boxing-an-ancient-tradition-a-necessary-skill, accessed June 7, 2011.

52. Curtis and Lang, 33.

53. Wiedemann, 156.

54. *Ancient Voices: "Gladiators: The Brutal Truth,"* (BBC History Documentary) BBC/A&E Co-Production, Time-Life Video Presentation, 2000.

CHAPTER 3

55. Jad Semaan, "Roman Gladiator Games: the Origins of MMA, Part Two," *Bleacher Report,* http://bleacherreport.com/articles/30004-roman-gladiator-games-the-origins-of-mma-part-two, accessed April 20, 2016.

56. *Gladiator Games: The Roman Bloodsport,* Prod. John Pattyson, et. al (TV 2000 Documentary), November 21, 2000.

57. Mark Cartwright, "Colosseum," *Ancient History Encyclopedia,* http://www.ancient.eu/Colosseum, accessed April 21, 2016.

58. Tim Constantine, "Selling baby body parts may kill abortion money machine," *The Washington Times,* http://www.washingtontimes.com/news/2015/jul/23/tim-constantine-selling-baby-body-parts-may-kill-a, accessed April 27, 2016.

59. "New Poll Reveals Evolution's Corrosive Impact on Beliefs about Human Uniqueness," *Evolution News,* http://www.evolutionnews.org/2016/04/new_poll_reveal102751.html, accessed April 21, 2016.

60. Hendricka Kuklick, ed., *New History of Anthropology* (Malden, MA: Blackwell Publishing, 2008), 229.

61. Guillemo Herrera, "UFC fighters are the Roman Gladiators of our time," *MemoRable,* http://supermemorable.blogspot.ca/2011/06/ufc-fighters-are-roman-gladiators-of.html?q=ufc, accessed April 20, 2016.

62. John McRay, *Archaeology & the New Testament* (Grand Rapids: Baker Academic, 2009), 62-63.

63. Micael Poliakoff, "Encyclopedia Britanica: Boxing," Britannica.com, http://www.britannica.com/sports/boxing, accessed April 20, 2016.

64. Jad Semaan, "Roman Gladiator Games: the Origins of MMA, Part One," *Bleacher Report,* http://bleacherreport.com/

articles/28473-ancient-greek-pankration-the-origins-of-mma-part-one, accessed April 20, 2016.

65. Ibid.

66. Christopher David Thrasher, *Fight Sports and American Masculinity: Salvation in Violence from 1609 to the Present* (North Carolina: McFarland & Company, Inc., 2015), 22.

67. Lorne Scoggins, "The History of Boxing Part 1: The Ancient Times," *Examiner.com*, http://www.examiner.com/article/the-history-of-boxing-part-1-the-ancient-times, accessed April 20, 2016.

68. Frank Daros, "Greek Pankratio," *Black Belt Magazine,* September 2004, 102.

69. Peter Hess, "The Development of Mixed Martial Arts: From Fighting Spectacles to State-Sanctioned Sporting Events," *Willamette Sports Law Journal* (2007), 9.

70. Ibid.

71. Dave Meltzer, "First UFC Forever Altered Combat Sports," *Yahoo Sports*, http://sports.yahoo.com/mma/news?slug=dm-earlyufc111207, accessed April 20, 2016.

72. Ibid.

73. Jack Encarnacao, "A Fighting Chance: College-educated Combatants Aim to Strike Blow for Mixed Martial Arts on New Reality TV Show." In Peter Hess, "The Development of Mixed Martial Arts," Boston Globe, January 15, 2005, 11.

74. Matthew Brennan, "Violence in Sports: Two more boxers die from head injuries," *World Socialist Web Site*, https://www.wsws.org/en/articles/2014/02/12/gonz-f12.html, accessed April 20, 2016.

75. "Boxing Should Be Banned," *American Public Health Association,* https://www.apha.org/policies-and-advocacy/public-health-policy-statements/policy-database/2014/07/08/18/05/boxing-should-be-banned,   accessed December 3, 2018.

76. Hess, 13.

77. Ibid, 23.

78. Michael David Smith, "UFC President Dana White: 'I Consider John McCain the Guy Who Started the UFC,'" *MMA Fighting,* https://www.mmafighting.com/2008/06/22/ufc-president-dana-white-i-consider-john-mccain-the-guy-who-st, accessed August 9, 2017.

79. Gary Holland, "History of London Boxing," *BBC News,* http://www.bbc.co.uk/london/content/articles/2007/11/13/early_boxing_history_feature.shtml, accessed April 20, 2016.

80. "Open Learn: Enlightenment," *The Open University, United Kingdom,* http://www.open.edu/openlearn/history-the-arts/history/history-art/the-enlightenment/content-section-7, accessed April 20, 2016.

81. Brett and Kate McKay, "Boxing: A Manly History of the Sweet Science of Bruising," *The Art of Manliness, Health & Sports,* http://www.artofmanliness.com/2009/05/30/boxing-a-manly-history-of-the-sweet-science-of-bruising, accessed April 20, 2016.

82. Boddy, Kasia, *Boxing: A Cultural History* (London: Reaktion Books Ltd., 2008), 27.

83. Nigel Collins, "Encyclopedia Britannica: Boxing Legal Issues," Britannica.com, http://www.britannica.com/sports/boxing/Boxings-legal-status, accessed April 20, 2016.

84. Thomas Hauser, "Encyclopedia Britannica: The Queensberry Rules," Britannica.com, http://www.britannica.com/sports/boxing/The-Queensberry-rules, accessed April 20, 2016.

85. Christianbook.com, https://www.christianbook.com/his-steps-what-would-jesus-do-charles-sheldon/9781935785163/pd/785163#CBD-PD-Publisher-Description, accessed December 3, 2018.

86. Charles M. Sheldon, *In His Steps,* Grand Rapids, MI: Kregal Publications, 2018, http://www.kregel.com/fiction/in-his-steps.

87. Charles M. Sheldon, *In His Steps*, Public Domain, What Saith the Scriptures. com https://www.whatsaiththescripture.com/Text.Only/pdfs/In.His.Steps. Text.pdf, 14-15.

88. William Blackstone, *Commentaries on the Laws of England* (Oxford: Clarendon Press, 1765-69), 4:183.

89. "Commonwealth vs. Benjamin F. Collberg. Same vs. Charles E. Phenix. Supreme Court of Massachusetts: 119 Mass. 350; 1876 Mass. LEXIS 350," *The Law of Self Defense*, https://lawofselfdefense.com/law_case/commonwealth-v-collberg-119-mass-350-ma-supreme-court-1876, accessed April 21, 2016.

90. Brett and Kate McKay, "Boxing: A Manly History of the Sweet Science of Bruising." *The Art of Manliness, Health & Sports,* http://www.artofmanliness. com/2009/05/30/boxing-a-manly-history-of-the-sweet-science-of-bruising, accessed August 23, 2017.

91. International Olympic Committee; *Olympic Studies Centre*. Boxing: History of Boxing at the Olympic Games, http://www.olympic.org/Assets/OSC%20 Section/pdf/QR_sports_summer/Sports_olympiques_boxe%20_eng.pdf, accessed April 21, 2016.

92. Tom Friend, "Boxing: A Heart-Rending Vigil after Tragedy in the Ring; Ruelas, Boxer Who Inflicted Injury, Prays With Family of Garcia, Now Battling for His Life," *New York Times*, http://www.nytimes.com/1995/05/19/sports/ boxing-heart-rending-vigil-after-tragedy-ring-ruelas-boxer-who-inflicted-injury.html, accessed April 21, 2016.

93. Ibid.

94. Shawn Murphy, "TSS Where are they now? Gabriel Ruelas," *The Sweet Science*, http://www.thesweetscience.com/article-archive/2010/11243-tss-where-are-they-now-gabriel-ruelas, accessed April 21, 2016.

95. Ibid.

96. Donald McRae, *Dark Trade: Lost in Boxing* (Edinburgh: Mainstream Publishing, 2013).

97. Ibid.

98. Mark Kriegel, "A Step Back: Families Continue to Heal 30 Years After Title Fight Between Ray Mancini and Duk-koo Kim," *New York Times*, http://www.nytimes.com/2012/09/17/sports/families-continue-to-heal-30-years-after-title-bout-between-ray-mancini-and-duk-koo-kim.html?_r=0, accessed April 21, 2016.

99. Ibid.

100. G.G. Fagan, *The Lure of the Arena: Social Psychology and the Crowd at the Roman Games* (Cambridge: Cambridge University Press, 2011), 286.

101. C. Darwin, *Descent of Man, and Selection in Relation to Sex* (London: John Murray, 1871), 1:100-101.

CHAPTER 4

102. "Fighting Politics," Dir. Emily Vahey, Film Documentary, 2009, https://www.youtube.com/watch?v=ddFbELpXTcg, accessed August 23, 2017.

103. R.M. Schneiderman, "Flock Is Now a Fight Team in Some Ministries," *New York Times*, February 1, 2010.

104. Ibid.

105. Ibid.

106. Adam Park, "Fight Church: A Film Review, and Some Thoughts on Evangelicals," *Sport in American History*, June 12, 2014.

107. Ibid.

108. Schneiderman, "Flock Is Now a Fight Team in Some Ministries."

109. Brett and Kate McKay, "Boxing: A Many History of the Sweet Science of Bruising," *The Art of Manliness, Health & Sports,* http://www.artofmanliness.

com/2009/05/30/boxing-a-manly-history-of-the-sweet-science-of-bruising, accessed August 23, 2017.

110. Schneiderman, "Flock Is Now a Fight Team in Some Ministries."

111. "MMA Fighting on SBN: Interview with Dana White on Romero's Post-Fight Comments," *MMA Fighting*, https://www.youtube.com/watch?v=p2Q8A4Pds1c#t=436, accessed August 23, 2017.

112. Monica Guzman, "Lynnwood 'Fight Pastor' Prepares to Take On the UFC," Seattlepi, December 9, 2009.

113. Tertullian, *The Shows* or *De Spectaculis*, Chapter 3, http://www.tertullian.org/anf/anf03/anf03-09.htm#P905_359143, accessed January 9, 2018.

114. Park, "Fight Church: A Film Review, and Some Thoughts on Evangelicals."

115. Ibid.

116. Ibid.

117. Mark Madden, "The Mark Madden Show," *WXDX Radio Pittsburgh*, https://www.youtube.com/watch?v=vRT-mdkjho8, accessed August 23, 2017.

118. Michael David Smith, "UFC 94 Video: B.J. Penn Tells Georges St. Pierre, 'I'm Going to Try to Kill You,'" *MMA Fighting*, http://www.mmafighting.com/2009/01/07/ufc-94-video-b-j-penn-tells-georges-st-pierre-im-going-to, accessed August 23, 2017.

119. David Doyle, "Florian Words for Penn Turn Heads," *Yahoo Sports*, http://sports.yahoo.com/mma/news?slug=dd-florian111608, accessed August 23, 2017.

120. William MacDonald, *Believer's Bible Commentary* (Nashville: Thomas Nelson Publishers, 1989), 561.

121. Saint Augustine, *The Confessions of St. Augustine,* translated by Edward Pusey. Vol. VII, Part 1. The Harvard Classics. New York: P.F. Collier & Son, 1909–14, http://www.bartleby.com/7/1/6.html, accessed January 9, 2018.

122. Theophilus, *Ante-Nicene Fathers* (Christian Classics Ethereal Library), 2:116, http://www.ccel.org/ccel/schaff/anf02.iv.ii.iii.xv.html, accessed August 23, 2017.

123. *Merriam-Webster's Dictionary, s.v.* "vicarious," accessed July 11, 2017, http://www.merriam-webster.com/dictionary/vicarious.

124. Leonard Sweet, *11: Indispensable Relationships You Can't Be Without,* (Colorado Springs: David C. Cook Publishing, 2012), 32.

CHAPTER 5

125. Sean Gregory, "Tragic Risks of American Football," *TIME Magazine,* September 29, 2014, 32.

126. "High School Football Player Dies From Tackle," *ABC News,* https://www.youtube.com/watch?v=78Ex9yH3qeA, accessed August 27, 2017.

127. Gregory, "Tragic Risks of American Football."

128. Review of *League of Denial,* by Mark Fainaru-Wada and Steve Fainaru, http://leagueofdenial.com/books/league-of-denial-tr, accessed May 16, 2019.

129. Shaoni Bhattacharya, "American Footballers Endure 'Car Crash' Blows," *New Scientist,* https://www.newscientist.com/article/dn4534-american-footballers-endure-car-crash-blows, accessed August 27, 2017.

130. Kyle G. Brown, "A Fight to the Death: Concussions in Wrestling," *Global News Beat,* http://www.globalnewsbeat.com/2008/02/04/a-fight-to-the-death-concussions-in-wrestling, accessed August 28, 2017.

131. Kelly Lyell, "Safety concerns prompt sharp drop in youth football participation," *Fort Collins Coloradoan,* https://www.coloradoan.com/story/sports/2018/09/03/safety-concerns-drop-youth-football-participation-us-colorado/1134593002, accessed December 3, 2018.

132. Paolo Bandini, "NFL concussion lawsuits explained," *The Guardian,* https://www.theguardian.com/sport/2013/aug/29/nfl-concussions-lawsuit-explained, accessed May 16, 2019.

133. NFL Concussion Settlement, https://www.nflconcussionsettlement. com, accessed May 16, 2019.

134. Bill Plaschke, "NFL's Modern-Day Gladiators Pay the Prices as the Crowd Roars," *L.A. Times,* http://www.latimes.com/sports/nfl/la-sp-0125-football-violence-plaschke-20150125-column.html#page=1, accessed August 28, 2017.

135. Jim Trotter, "Depression Prevalent in Ex-players," *ESPN,* http://www.espn. com/nfl/story/_/page/hotread150225/depression-suicide-raise-issue-mental-health-former-nfl-players, accessed August 28, 2017.

136. Lyell.

137. Katie Zezima, "How Teddy Roosevelt helped save football," *Washington Post,* https://www.washingtonpost.com/news/the-fix/wp/2014/05/29/teddy-roosevelt-helped-save-football-with-a-white-house-meeting-in-1905/?utm_term=.e56cb6933679, accessed July 11, 2017.

138. Garry Wills, "Bloodlust and the Superbowl," *New York Review Daily,* http://www.nybooks.com/daily/2011/02/04/blood-lust-and-super-bowl, accessed August 28, 2017.

139. Bruce Dowbiggin, "Mike Milbury Sees the Light," *Globe and Mail,* http://www.theglobeandmail.com/sports/hockey/mike-milbury-sees-the-light/article623700, accessed August 28, 2017.

140. Allan Maki, "Corey Fulton Works His Way Back From Hockey Tragedy," *Globe and Mail,* https://www.theglobeandmail.com/sports/corey-fulton-works-his-way-back-from-hockey-tragedy/article1320327, accessed August 28, 2017.

141. Lyell.

142. "High School Football Player Dies From Tackle," *ABC News.*

143. Lyell.

144. Lisa Rapaport, "Fewer U.S. high school athletes play football amid concussion fears," *Reuters,* https://www.reuters.com/article/us-health-kids-tackle-football/

fewer-u-s-high-school-athletes-play-football-amid-concussion-fears-idUSKCN1GO2LY, accessed December 3, 2018.

145. Roy MacGregor, "Concussion concerns fuel desire for youth hockey bodychecking ban: Survey," *Globe and Mail*, https://www.theglobeandmail.com/sports/hockey/concussion-concerns-fuel-desire-for-youth-hockey-bodychecking-ban-survey/article9255518, accessed August 28, 2017.

146. Callie Caplan, "Lawrence Taylor jokes that he did Joe Theismann a favor by ending his career," *USA TODAY Sports*, https://www.usatoday.com/story/sports/nfl/2016/06/16/lawrence-taylor-joe-theismann/86001078, accessed January 3, 2018.

147. Leonard Shapiro, "The Hit That Changed a Career," *Washington Post*, http://www.washingtonpost.com/wp-dyn/content/article/2005/11/17/AR2005111701635.html, accessed January 3, 2018.

148. Pat Leonard, "Giants legend Lawrence Taylor on Joe Theismann: 'I did him a favor,'" *New York Daily News*, http://www.nydailynews.com/sports/football/giants/giants-legend-lt-joe-theismann-favor-article-1.2682164, accessed January 3, 2018.

149. Caplan, "Lawrence Taylor jokes that he did Joe Theismann a favor by ending his career."

150. Joel Thorman, "Eric Winston: Fans cheering Matt Cassel's injury are 'sickening,'" *Arrowhead Pride*, https://www.arrowheadpride.com/2012/10/7/3470224/eric-winston-quotes-matt-cassel-injury-fans-cheering, accessed January 3, 2018.

151. Ibid.

152. "MMA Documentary." Evan Solomon, *CBC News*: Canada, May 28, 2006.

153. "History of Gladiators," *Imperial Romans of New Zealand*, http://www.imperium-romana.org/history-of-gladiators.html, accessed July 12, 2017.

154. James Grout, "The Roman Gladiator," *Encyclopaedia Romana*, 1997-2017, http://penelope.uchicago.edu/~grout/encyclopaedia_romana/gladiators/gladiators.html, accessed August 28, 2017.

155. Keith Hopkins, "Murderous Games: Gladiatorial Contests in Ancient Rome," *History Today*, Volume 33, Issue 6, June 1983, http://www.historytoday.com/keith-hopkins/murderous-games-gladiatorial-contests-ancient-rome, accessed August 28, 2017.

156. Josh Visser, *CTV.ca News Staff*, July 11, 2009.

157. "Boxing," *British Medical Association*, June 4, 2008, http://www.bma.org.uk/health_promotion_ethics/sports_exercise/boxing.jsp, accessed January 28, 2010.

158. World Medical Association Statement on Boxing, https://www.wma.net/policies-post/wma-statement-on-boxing, accessed August 28, 2017. Website updated with new policy statement November 12, 2018.

159. "WMA Statement on Boxing," *World Medical Association*, https://www.wma.net/policies-post/wma-statement-on-boxing, accessed December 3, 2018.

160. "Boxing," *British Medical Association.*

161. "Should we ban boxing?" *BMJ*, http://www.bmj.com/content/352/bmj.i389, accessed January 3, 2018.

162. Tom Blackwell, "MMA Fighters Suffer Traumatic Brain Injury In Almost a Third of Professional Bouts: Study," *National Post*, http://news.nationalpost.com/news/canada/mma-fighters-suffer-traumatic-brain-injury-in-almost-a-third-of-professional-bouts-study, accessed August 28, 2017.

163. Gregory H. Bledsoe, Edbert B. Hsu etc. "Incidence of Injury in Professional Mixed Martial Arts Competitions," *Journal of Sports Science and Medicine*, 136-142, http://www.ncbi.nlm.nih.gov/pmc/articles/PMC3863915, accessed August 28, 2017.

164. Jim Murray, "'He Can Take It' and Not Make It," *L.A. Times*, http://articles.latimes.com/1995-11-30/sports/sp-8615_1_gabriel-ruelas, accessed July 11, 2017.

165. "Boxing," *British Medical Association.*

166. Gregory.

167. Hannah Karp, "What's the Point of Cheerleading? As Studies Suggest It's Dangerous, Some Schools Rethink Teams; the Pyramid Ban," Wall Street Journal, https://www.wsj.com/articles/SB10001424052970204518504574417392008401168, accessed August 28, 2017.

168. "Health Topics: Violence," World Health Organization, http://www.who.int/topics/violence/en, accessed July 17, 2017.

169. Dictionary.com, s.v. "violate," http://www.dictionary.com/browse/violate, accessed July 12, 2017.

170. Sean O'Neil, "Christianity's Concussion Crisis: Where Football and Faith Collide," *Religion Dispatches*, http://religiondispatches.org/christianitys-concussion-crisis-where-football-and-faith-collide, accessed August 28, 2017.

171. Tom Krattenmaker, "NFL Violence a Moral Thorn for Christians," *USA Today*, https://www.usatoday.com/story/opinion/2013/10/09/nfl-concussions-football-christians-column/2955997, accessed August 28, 2017.

172. Garry Wills, "Bloodlust and the Superbowl," *New York Review Daily*, http://www.nybooks.com/daily/2011/02/04/blood-lust-and-super-bowl,accessed July 11, 2017.

CHAPTER 6

173. National Churchill Museum, "Those who fail to learn from history . . . ," https://www.nationalchurchillmuseum.org/blog/churchill-quote-history, accessed June 7, 2017.

174. Matt Connolly, "New York To Legalize MMA: Why It Took So Long, And What It Means Going Forward," *Forbes,* https://www.forbes.com/sites/mattconnolly/2016/03/23/new-york-to-legalize-mma-why-it-took-so-long-and-what-it-means-going-forward/#1fc785703abc, accessed June 7, 2017.

175. Louise Roseingrave, "MMA fighter Joao Carvalho died due to blunt force trauma," *Irish Times,* https://www.irishtimes.com/news/crime-and-law/

courts/coroner-s-court/mma-fighter-joao-carvalho-died-due-to-blunt-force-trauma-1.2907231, accessed June 7, 2017.

176. Reid Forgrave, "MMA, Olympics perfect bedfellows," Foxsports.com, http://www.foxsports.com/ufc/story/mma-could-be-added-to-2020-olympics-dana-white-combat-sports-073112, accessed June 7, 2017.

177. Joan Alker, "Children in the Dawn and Shadows of Life Should be a Top Priority in Budget Talks," *Georgetown University Health Policy Institute*, https://ccf.georgetown.edu/2011/07/14/children_in_the_dawn_and_shadows_of_life_should_be_a_top_priority_in_budget_talks, accessed June 7, 2017.

178. "Cage-Fighting Kids," *ABC News*, https://www.youtube.com/watch?v=4yy-QlFXOro, accessed July 11, 2017.

Some might question a child losing four pounds in two days (as in the short fiction story of Avalanche); but in this news report, one young ten-year-old girl lost five pounds in two days.

179. Jim Norman, "Views of US Moral Values Slip to Seven-Year Lows," *Gallup*, http://www.gallup.com/poll/210917/views-moral-values-slip-seven-year-lows.aspx, accessed June 7, 2017.

180. "Exploring the Dark World of Children's MMA," *Huff Post Live Show*, http://live.huffingtonpost.com/r/segment/mixed-martial-arts-for-children/52794a3e02a7601a9e00010b, accessed June 7, 2017.

181. "Cage-Fighting Kids," *ABC News*.

182. Bob Moffitt, "California Kids Prepare For Steel Cage Matches," *Capital Public Radio*, http://www.capradio.org/articles/2015/08/14/california-kids-prepare-for-steel-cage-matches, accessed February 11, 2019.

183. News 10 Staff and KXTV, "Kids MMA continues to grow despite state shutdown," *abc10*, https://www.abc10.com/article/news/kids-mma-continues-to-grow-despite-state-shutdown/310212283, accessed February 11, 2019.

184. Becky Little, "Photos Show Controversial World of Kids' Mixed Martial Arts Fighting," *National Geographic*, https://news.nationalgeographic.com/2016/07/pictures-kids-mixed-martial-arts-sports, accessed February 11, 2019.

185. Brett Okamoto, "Ronda Rousey considered suicide after loss to Holly Holm," *ESPN*, http://www.espn.com/mma/story/_/id/14785901/ronda-rousey-says-considered-suicide-loss-holly-holm, accessed July 11, 2017.

186. Sam Caplan, "MMA For Kids, You've Got To Be Kidding Me," *Five Ounces of Pain*, http://www.fiveouncesofpain.com/2008/03/31/mma-for-kids-youve-got-to-be-kidding-me, accessed July 11, 2017.

187. "WMA Statement on Boxing," *World Medical Association*, November 12, 2018, https://www.wma.net/policies-post/wma-statement-on-boxing, accessed December 3, 2018.

188. *Gladiators: Back From the Dead,* (TV Documentary).

189. Albert Mohler, "It Takes a Church Focused on the Family of God," *The Gospel Coalition,* https://www.youtube.com/watch?v=6gXMJcSIo9k 3:17, accessed May 16, 2019.

190. John Walton, "The Four Kingdoms of Daniel," *JETS* 29/1 (March 1986) 25-36, http://www.etsjets.org/files/JETS-PDFs/29/29-1/29-1-pp025-036_JETS.pdf, accessed August 28, 2017.

191. "Four Kingdoms of Daniel," *Wikipedia*, https://en.wikipedia.org/wiki/Four_kingdoms_of_Daniel, accessed July 12, 2017. Notes: The traditional interpretation of the four kingdoms, shared among Jewish and Christian expositors for over two millennia, identifies the kingdoms as the empires of Babylon, Medo-Persia, Greece, and Rome. This view conforms to the text of Daniel, which considers the Medo-Persian Empire as one, as with the "law of the Medes and Persians." These views have the support of the Jewish Talmud; medieval Jewish commentators; and Christian church fathers, Jerome and Calvin.

192. Gill's Exposition of the Entire Bible, "Daniel 2:35," *Bible Hub*, https://biblehub.com/commentaries/daniel/2-35.htm, accessed May 16, 2019.

193. Bill O'Reilly, "The O'Reilly Factor," *Fox News*, 2006.

194. Mihai Andrei, "Company wants to resurrect gladiators – with a modern twist," *ZME Science*, http://www.zmescience.com/other/feature-post/modern-gladiator-competition, accessed August 28, 2017.

195. Edwin Kee, "Unified Weapons Master Brings Us Back to the Colosseum," *Ubergizmo*, http://www.ubergizmo.com/2015/04/unified-weapons-master-brings-us-back-to-the-colosseum, accessed August 28, 2017.

196. Aaron Crossman, "Unified Weapons Master brings the world of martial combat sports with weaponry!," *Computer America*, http://computeramerica.com/2015/05/23/unified-weapons-masters-brings-the-world-martial-combat-sports-with-weaponry, accessed August 28, 2017.

197. Jonathan Wells, "Knight fights: Inside the strange and savage world of medieval MMA," *The Telegraph*, http://www.telegraph.co.uk/men/the-filter/knight-fights-inside-the-strange-and-savage-world-of-medieval-mm, accessed January 9, 2018.

198. "Battle of the Nations: World Historical Medieval Battle Championship," *Cision*, http://www.newswire.ca/news-releases/battle-of-the-nations-world-historical-medieval-battle-championship-511218031.html, accessed January 3, 2018.

199. "Battle of the Nations: World Championship in Historical Medieval Battle" website, http://botn.devlits.com/en#tournament, accessed January 3, 2018.

200. G.G. Fagan, *The Lure of the Arena: Social Psychology and the Crowd at the Roman Games* (Cambridge: Cambridge University Press, 2011), 286.

201. Ibid.

202. Matthew Naismith. "If it was allowed would an arena with gladiators fighting to the death prove popular in modern times?" *TED*, There were just

under 40 respondents, http://www.ted.com/conversations/17536/if_it_was_allowed_would_an_are.html, accessed August 28, 2017.

203. Ibid.

204. Ibid.

205. Jesse Hicks, "Probing Question: Is football similar to Roman Gladiator Games?," *Penn State News,* http://news.psu.edu/story/141233/2009/09/14/research/probing-question-football-similar-roman-gladiator-games, accessed August 28, 2017.

206. Ibid.

207. *Gladiator Games: The Roman Bloodsport,* Prod. John Pattyson, et. al (TV Documentary), November 21, 2000.

208. Ibid.

209. John Oswalt, *The Book of Isaiah: Chapters 1-39* (Grand Rapids: Eerdmans Publishing Co., 1986), 396.

210. *Gladiator Games: Roman Blood Sport.* Exec. Prod. John Pattyson, et al. (2000, Glendale, CA: DreamWorks, November 21, 2000), TV.

BIBLIOGRAPHY

Alker, Joan. "Children in the Dawn and Shadows of Life Should be a Top Priority in Budget Talks." *Georgetown University Health Policy Institute.* https://ccf.georgetown.edu/2011/07/14/children_in_the_dawn_and_shadows_of_life_should_be_a_top_priority_in_budget_talks (accessed June 7, 2017).

Ancient Voices: "Gladiators: The Brutal Truth." BBC/A&E Co-Production, Time-Life Video Presentation, 2000.

Andrei, Mihai. "Company wants to resurrect gladiators—with a modern twist." *ZME Science,* http://www.zmescience.com/other/feature-post/modern-gladiator-competition (accessed August 28, 2017).

Augustine, Saint. *The Confessions of St. Augustine.* Translated by Edward Pusey. Vol. VII, Part 1. The Harvard Classics New York: P.F. Collier & Son, 1909–14. http://www.bartleby.com/7/1/6.html (accessed January 9, 2018).

Bandini, Paolo. "NFL concussion lawsuits explained." *The Guardian.* https://www.theguardian.com/sport/2013/aug/29/nfl-concussions-lawsuit-explained (accessed May 16, 2019).

"Battle of the Nations: World Championship in Historical Medieval Battle." http://botn.devlits.com/en#tournament (accessed January 3, 2018).

"Battle of the Nations: World Historical Medieval Battle Championship." Cision. http://www.newswire.ca/news-releases/battle-of-the-nations-world-historical-medieval-battle-championship-511218031.html (accessed January 3, 2018).

Bhattacharya, Shaoni. "American Footballers Endure 'Car Crash' Blows." *New Scientist.* https://www.newscientist.com/article/dn4534-american-footballers-endure-car-crash-blows (accessed August 27, 2017).

Blackstone, William. *Commentaries on the Laws of England.* Oxford: Clarendon Press, 1765-69. 4:183.

Blackwell, Tom. "MMA Fighters Suffer Traumatic Brain Injury in Almost a Third of Professional Bouts: Study." *National Post.* http://news.nationalpost.com/news/canada/mma-fighters-suffer-traumatic-brain-injury-in-almost-a-third-of-professional-bouts-study (accessed August 28, 2017).

Bledsoe, Gregory H., et al. "Incidence of Injury in Professional Mixed Martial Arts Competitions." *Journal of Sports Science and Medicine,* July 5, 2006. 136-142. http://www.ncbi.nlm.nih.gov/pmc/articles/PMC3863915 (accessed August 28, 2017).

Boddy, Kasia. *Boxing: A Cultural History.* London: Reaktion Books Ltd., 2008. 27.

"Boxing: An Ancient Tradition, A Necessary Skill." Boxing Herald.com. http://www.boxingherald.com/boxing-news/boxing-an-ancient-tradition-a-necessary-skill (accessed June 7, 2011).

"Boxing." *British Medical Association.* http://www.bma.org.uk/health_promotion_ethics/sports_exercise/boxing.jsp (accessed January 28, 2010).

"Boxing Should Be Banned," *American Public Health Association.* https://www.apha.org/policies-and-advocacy/public-health-policy-statements/policy-database/2014/07/08/18/05/boxing-should-be-banned (accessed December 3, 2018).

Brennan, Matthew. "Violence in Sports: Two more boxers die from head injuries." *World Socialist Web Site.* https://www.wsws.org/en/articles/2014/02/12/gonz-f12.html (accessed April 20, 2016).

Brown, Josh. "Hominick Stole the Show at UFC 129." *The Record.* http://www.therecord.com/sports/local/article/531955—hominick-stole-the-show-at-ufc-129 (accessed April 25, 2016).

Brown, Kyle G. "A Fight to the Death: Concussions in Wrestling." *Global News Beat* http://www.globalnewsbeat.com/2008/02/04/a-fight-to-the-death-concussions-in-wrestling (accessed August 28, 2017).

Buffery, Steve. "St. Pierre Stars but Hominick Steals the Show." *Toronto Sun*. http://www.torontosun.com/2011/05/01/   st-pierre-stars-but-hominick-steals-the-show (accessed June 12, 2011).

"Cage-Fighting Kids." *ABC News*. https://www.youtube.com/watch?v=4yy-QlFXOr0 (accessed July 11, 2017).

Caplan, Callie. "Lawrence Taylor jokes that he did Joe Theismann a favor by ending his career." *USA TODAY Sports*. https://www.usatoday.com/story/sports/nfl/2016/06/16/lawrence-taylor-joe-theismann/86001078 (accessed January 3, 2018).

Caplan, Sam. *"MMA For Kids? You've Got To Be Kidding Me!" Five Ounces of Pain*. http://www.fiveouncesofpain.com/2008/03/31/mma-for-kids-youve-got-to-be-kidding-me (accessed July 11, 2017).

Cartwright, Mark. "Colosseum." *Ancient History Encyclopedia*. http://www.ancient.eu/Colosseum (accessed April 21, 2016).

Chadwick, H. *The Early Church*. New York: Penguin Books, 1967. 56.

Connolly, Matt. "New York To Legalize MMA: Why It Took So Long, And What It Means Going Forward." *Forbes*. https://www.forbes.com/sites/mattconnolly/2016/03/23/new-york-to-legalize-mma-why-it-took-so-long-and-what-it-means-going-forward/#1fc785703abc (accessed June 7, 2017).

Collins, Nigel. "Encyclopedia Britannica: Boxing Legal Issues." *Britannica.com*. http://www.britannica.com/sports/boxing/Boxings-legal-status (accessed April 20, 2016).

"Commonwealth vs. Benjamin F. Collberg. Same vs. Charles E. Phenix. Supreme Court Of Massachusetts: 119 Mass. 350; 1876 Mass. LEXIS 350." *The Law of Self Defense*. https://lawofselfdefense.com/law_case/commonwealth-v-collberg-119-mass-350-ma-supreme-court-1876 (accessed April 21, 2016).

Constantine, Tim. "Selling baby body parts may kill abortion money machine." *The Washington Times.* http://www.washingtontimes.com/news/2015/jul/23/tim-constantine-selling-baby-body-parts-may-kill-a (accessed April 27, 2016).

Crossman, Aaron. "Unified Weapons Master brings the world of martial combat sports with weaponry!" *Computer America.* http://computeramerica.com/2015/05/23/unified-weapons-masters-brings-the-world-martial-combat-sports-with-weaponry (accessed August 28, 2017).

Curtis, A. and J. Lang. *Dates with Destiny.* New York: Fleming H. Revel Company, 1991. 24.

Daros, Frank. "Greek Pankratio." *Black Belt Magazine,* September 2004. 102.

Darwin, C. *Descent of Man, and Selection in Relation to Sex.* London: John Murray, 1871. 1:100-101.

Deibert, D. "Brain Hemorrhage Forces Brian Foster off UFC 129 in Toronto." *Vancouver Sun,* April 12, 2011.

Dictionary.com, s.v. "violate," http://www.dictionary.com/browse/violate (accessed July 12, 2017).

Dowbiggin, Bruce. "Mike Milbury Sees the Light." *Globe and Mail.* http://www.theglobeandmail.com/sports/hockey/mike-milbury-sees-the-light/article623700 (accessed August 28, 2017).

Doyle, David. "Florian Words for Penn Turn Heads." *Yahoo Sports.* http://sports.yahoo.com/mma/news?slug=dd-florian111608 (accessed August 23, 2017).

"Exploring the Dark World of Children's MMA." *Huff Post Live Show.* http://live.huffingtonpost.com/r/segment/mixed-martial-arts-for-children/52794a3e02a7601a9e00010b (accessed June 7, 2017).

Fagan, G.G. *The Lure of the Arena: Social Psychology and the Crowd at the Roman Games.* Cambridge: Cambridge University Press, 2011. 156-315.

"Fighting Politics." Directed by Emily Vahey. Film Documentary, 2009. https://www.youtube.com/watch?v=ddFbELpXTcg (accessed August 23, 2017).

Forgrave, Reid. "MMA, Olympics perfect bedfellows." *Foxsports.com.* http://www.foxsports.com/ufc/story/mma-could-be-added-to-2020-olympics-dana-white-combat-sports-073112 (accessed June 7, 2017).

"Four Kingdoms of Daniel." *Wikipedia.* https://en.wikipedia.org/wiki/Four_kingdoms_of_Daniel (accessed July 12, 2017).

Friend, Tom. "Boxing: A Heart-Rending Vigil after Tragedy in the Ring; Ruelas, Boxer Who Inflicted Injury, Prays With Family of Garcia, Now Battling for His Life." *New York Times.* http://www.nytimes.com/1995/05/19/sports/boxing-heart-rending-vigil-after-tragedy-ring-ruelas-boxer-who-inflicted-injury.html (accessed April 21, 2016).

Futrell, A. *The Roman Games.* Malden, MA: Blackwell Publishing, 2006. 62.

Gill's Exposition of the Entire Bible. "Daniel 2:35." Bible Hub, https://biblehub.com/commentaries/daniel/2-35.htm (accessed May 16, 2019).

"Gladiator." *Merriam-Webster Dictionary.* http://www.merriam-webster.com/dictionary/gladiator (accessed June 12, 2011).

Gladiators: Back From the Dead. Directed by Jeremy Turner. 2010. Channel 4, TV Documentary. London, England, June 14, 2010..

Gladiator Games: Roman Blood Sport. Exec. Prod. John Pattyson, et al. 2000. Glendale, CA: DreamWorks, November 21, 2000. TV.

Gregory, Sean. "Tragic Risks of American Football." *TIME Magazine,* September 29, 2014. 32.

Grout, James. "The Roman Gladiator." *Encyclopaedia Romana,* 1997-2017. http://penelope.uchicago.edu/~grout/encyclopaedia_romana/gladiators/gladiators.html (accessed August 28, 2017).

Guzman, Monica. "Lynnwood 'Fight Pastor' Prepares to Take On the UFC." Seattlepi, https://www.seattlepi.com/local/article/Lynnwood-Fight-Pastor-prepares-to-take-on-the-894227.php (accessed October 26, 2018).

Hauser, Thomas. "Encyclopedia Britannica: The Queensberry Rules." Britannica. com. http://www.britannica.com/sports/boxing/The-Queensberry-rules (accessed April 20, 2016).

"Health Topics: Violence." World Health Organization. http://www.who.int/topics/violence/en (accessed July 17, 2017).

Herrera, Guillemo. "UFC fighters are the Roman Gladiators of our time." MemoRable. http://supermemorable.blogspot.ca/2011/06/ufc-fighters-are-roman-gladiators-of.html?q=ufc (accessed April 20, 2016).

Hess, Peter. "The Development of Mixed Martial Arts: From Fighting Spectacles to State-Sanctioned Sporting Events." *Willamette Sports Law Journal*, 2007. 9, 11.

Hicks, Jesse. "Probing Question: Is football similar to Roman Gladiator Games?" *Penn State News*. http://news.psu.edu/story/141233/2009/09/14/research/probing-question-football-similar-roman-gladiator-games (accessed August 28, 2017).

"High School Football Player Dies From Tackle." *ABC News*. https://www.youtube.com/watch?v=78Ex9yH3qeA (accessed August 27, 2017).

"History of Gladiators." *Imperial Romans of New Zealand*. http://www.imperium-romana.org/history-of-gladiators.html (accessed July 12, 2017).

Holland, Gary. "History of London Boxing." *BBC News* http://www.bbc.co.uk/london/content/articles/2007/11/13/early_boxing_history_feature.shtml (accessed April 20, 2016).

Hopkins, Keith. "Murderous Games: Gladiatorial Contests in Ancient Rome." *History Today*, Volume 33, Issue 6, June 1983. http://www.historytoday.com/keith-hopkins/murderous-games-gladiatorial-contests-ancient-rome (accessed August 28, 2017).

Hoye, Russel et al. *Sport Management: Principles and Application.* New York: Routledge 2015, 12:3.

International Olympic Committee; Olympic Studies Centre. Boxing: History of Boxing at the Olympic Games. http://www.olympic.org/Assets/OSC%20 Section/pdf/QR_sports_summer/Sports_olympiques_boxe%20_eng.pdf (accessed April 21, 2016).

Jacobelli, L, *Gladiators at Pompeii.* Los Angeles: Getty Publications, 2003. 39-102.

Karp, Hannah. "What's the Point of Cheerleading? As Studies Suggest It's Dangerous, Some Schools Rethink Teams; the Pyramid Ban." *Wall Street Journal.* https://www.wsj.com/articles/SB100014240529702045185045744173 92008401168 (accessed August 28, 2017).

Kee, Edwin. "Unified Weapons Master Brings Us Back to the Colosseum." *Ubergizmo.* http://www.ubergizmo.com/2015/04/unified-weapons-master-brings-us-back-to-the-colosseum (accessed August 28, 2017).

Krattenmaker, Tom. "NFL Violence a Moral Thorn for Christians." *USA Today.* https://www.usatoday.com/story/opinion/2013/10/09/nfl-concussions-football-christians-column/2955997 (accessed August 28, 2017).

Kriegel, Mark. "A Step Back: Families Continue to Heal 30 Years After Title Fight Between Ray Mancini and Duk-koo Kim." *New York Times.* http://www.nytimes.com/2012/09/17/sports/families-continue-to-heal-30-years-after-title-bout-between-ray-mancini-and-duk-koo-kim.html?_r=0 (accessed April 21, 2016).

Kuklick, Hendricka, ed. *New History of Anthropology.* Malden, MA: Blackwell Publishing, 2008. 229.

Leonard, Pat. "Giants legend Lawrence Taylor on Joe Theismann: 'I did him a favor.'" *New York Daily News.* http://www.nydailynews.com/sports/football/giants/giants-legend-lt-joe-theismann-favor-article-1.2682164 (accessed January 3, 2018).

Lyell, Kelly. "Safety concerns prompt sharp drop in youth football participation." *Fort Collins Coloradoan*. https://www.coloradoan.com/story/sports/2018/09/03/safety-concerns-drop-youth-football-participation-us-colorado/1134593002 (accessed December 3, 2018).

MacDonald, William. *Believer's Bible Commentary*. Nashville: Thomas Nelson Publishers, 1989. 561.

MacGregor, Roy. "Concussion concerns fuel desire for youth hockey bodychecking ban: Survey." *Globe and Mail*. https://www.theglobeandmail.com/sports/hockey/concussion-concerns-fuel-desire-for-youth-hockey-bodychecking-ban-survey/article9255518 (accessed August 28, 2017).

Madden, Mark. "The Mark Madden Show." *WXDX Radio Pittsburgh*. https://www.youtube.com/watch?v=vRT-mdkjho8 (accessed August 23, 2017).

Maki, Allan. "Corey Fulton Works His Way Back From Hockey Tragedy." *Globe and Mail*. https://www.theglobeandmail.com/sports/corey-fulton-works-his-way-back-from-hockey-tragedy/article1320327 (accessed August 28, 2017).

McKay, Brett and Kate. "Boxing: A Manly History of the Sweet Science of Bruising." *The Art of Manliness, Health & Sports*. http://www.artofmanliness.com/2009/05/30/boxing-a-manly-history-of-the-sweet-science-of-bruising (accessed April 20, 2016).

McRae, Donald. *Dark Trade: Lost in Boxing*. Edinburgh: Mainstream Publishing, 2013.

McRay, John. *Archaeology & the New Testament*. Grand Rapids: Baker Academic, 2009. 62-63.

Meltzer, Dave. "First UFC Forever Altered Combat Sports." *Yahoo Sports*. http://sports.yahoo.com/mma/news?slug=dm-earlyufc111207 (accessed April 20, 2016).

Merriam-Webster's Dictionary, s.v. "vicarious." http://www.merriam-webster.com/dictionary/vicarious (accessed July 11, 2017).

Merriam-Webster Dictionary, s.v. "vicariously." http://www.merriam-webster.com/dictionary/vicariously (accessed April 20, 2016).

"MMA Documentary." Evan Solomon, *CBC News*: Canada, May 28, 2006.

"MMA Fighting on SBN: Interview with Dana White on Romero's Post-Fight Comments." *MMA Fighting*. https://www.youtube.com/watch?v=p2Q8A4Pds1c#t=436 (accessed August 23, 2017).

Mohler, Albert. "It Takes a Church Focused on the Family of God." *The Gospel Coalition*. https://www.youtube.com/watch?v=6gXMJcSIo9k 3:17 (accessed May 16, 2019).

Murphy, Shawn. "TSS Where are they now? Gabriel Ruelas." *The Sweet Science*. http://www.thesweetscience.com/article-archive/2010/11243-tss-where-are-they-now-gabriel-ruelas (accessed April 21, 2016).

Murray, Jim. "'He Can Take It' and Not Make It." *L.A. Times*. http://articles.latimes.com/1995-11-30/sports/sp-8615_1_gabriel-ruelas (accessed July 11, 2017).

Naismith, Matthew. "If it was allowed would an arena with gladiators fighting to the death prove popular in modern times?" *TED*. http://www.ted.com/conversations/17536/if_it_was_allowed_would_an_are.html   (accessed August 28, 2017).

National Churchill Museum. "Those who fail to learn from history ..." https://www.nationalchurchillmuseum.org/blog/churchill-quote-history (accessed June 7, 2017).

"New Poll Reveals Evolution's Corrosive Impact on Beliefs about Human Uniqueness." *Evolution News*. http://www.evolutionnews.org/2016/04/new_poll_reveal102751.html (accessed April 21, 2016).

NFL Concussion Settlement. https://www.nflconcussionsettlement.com/ (accessed May 16, 2019).

Norman, Jim. "Views of US Moral Values Slip to Seven-Year Lows." *Gallup*. http://www.gallup.com/poll/210917/views-moral-values-slip-seven-year-lows.aspx (accessed June 7, 2017).

Okamoto, Brett. "Ronda Rousey considered suicide after loss to Holly Holm." *ESPN.* *http://www.espn.com/mma/story/_/id/14785901/ronda-rousey-says-considered-suicide-loss-holly-holm* (accessed July 11, 2017).

O'Neil, Sean. "Christianity's Concussion Crisis: Where Football and Faith Collide." *Religion Dispatches.* http://religiondispatches.org/christianitys-concussion-crisis-where-football-and-faith-collide (accessed August 28, 2017).

"Open Learn: Enlightenment." *The Open University, United Kingdom.* http://www.open.edu/openlearn/history-the-arts/history/history-art/the-enlightenment/content-section-7 (accessed April 20, 2016).

O'Reilly, Bill. "The O'Reilly Factor." *Fox News,* 2006.

Oswalt, John. *The Book of Isaiah: Chapters 1-39.* Grand Rapids: Eerdmans Publishing Co., 1986. 396.

Park, Adam. "Fight Church: A Film Review, and Some Thoughts on Evangelicals." *Sport in American History,* 2014.

Peterson, Kristen. "The Art in UFC's Violence." *Las Vegas Sun.* http://www.lasvegassun.com/news/2008/may/22/art-ufcs-violence (accessed April 20, 2016).

Plaschke, Bill. "NFL's Modern-Day Gladiators Pay the Prices as the Crowd Roars." *L.A. Times.* http://www.latimes.com/sports/nfl/la-sp-0125-football-violence-plaschke-20150125-column.html#page=1 (accessed August 28, 2017).

Poliakoff, Micael. "Encyclopedia Britannica: Boxing." Britannica.com. http://www.britannica.com/sports/boxing (accessed April 20, 2016).

Rapaport, Lisa. "Fewer U.S. high school athletes play football amid concussion fears." *Reuters.* March 12, 2018. https://www.reuters.com/article/us-health-kids-tackle-football/fewer-us-high-school-athletes-play-football-amid-concussion-fears-idUSKCN1GO2LY (accessed December 3, 2018).

Review of *League of Denial.* http://leagueofdenial.com/books/league-of-denial-tr (accessed May 16, 2019).

Roberts, A. and J. Donaldson, ed. "Theophilus of Antioch." *Ante-Nicene Fathers*, 2.223. In Ages Software, Oregon, 1997.

Roberts, A. and J. Donaldson, ed. "Irenaus: Against Heresies." *Ante-Nicene Fathers*, 1. 1. 3. 641. In Ages Software, Oregon, 1997.

Roberts, A. and J. Donaldson, ed. "Address of Tatian to the Greeks." *Ante-Nicene Fathers*, 2. 1. 138. In Ages Software, Oregon, 1997.

Roberts, A. and J. Donaldson, ed. "Latin Christianity: Its Founder, Tertullian," *Ante-Nicene Fathers*, 3.19. 160, In Ages Software, Oregon, 1997.

Roseingrave, Louise. "MMA fighter Joao Carvalho died due to blunt force trauma." *Irish Times*. https://www.irishtimes.com/news/crime-and-law/courts/coroner-s-court/mma-fighter-joao-carvalho-died-due-to-blunt-force-trauma-1.2907231 (accessed June 7, 2017).

Rothstein, E. "Shelf Life; A Bioethicist's Take on Genesis." *The New York Times*. http://www.nytimes.com/2003/08/02/arts/02SHEL.html (accessed April 20, 2016).

Schaff, Phillip and Henry Wace. *A Select Library of Nicene and Post-Nicene Fathers of the Christian Church*. Chapter 26. Vol. 3. New York: The Christian Literature Company, 1892, 151.

Schneiderman, R.M. "Flock Is Now a Fight Team in Some Ministries." *New York Times*, February 1, 2010.

Scoggins, Lorne. "The History of Boxing Part 1: The Ancient Times." *Examiner.com*. http://www.examiner.com/article/the-history-of-boxing-part-1-the-ancient-times (accessed April 20, 2016).

Semaan, Jad. "Roman Gladiator Games: The Origins of MMA, Part One." *Bleacher Report*. http://bleacherreport.com/articles/28473-ancient-greek-pankration-the-origins-of-mma-part-one (accessed April 20, 2016).

Semaan, Jad. "Roman Gladiator Games: The Origins of MMA, Part Two." *Bleacher Report*. http://bleacherreport.com/articles/30004-roman-gladiator-games-the-origins-of-mma-part-two (accessed April 20, 2016).

Shapiro, Leonard. "The Hit That Changed a Career." *Washington Post.* http://www.washingtonpost.com/wpdyn/content/article/2005/11/17/AR2005111701635.html (accessed January 3, 2018).

Sheldon, Charles M. *In His Steps.* Grand Rapids, MI: Kregal Publications, 2018. http://www.kregel.com/fiction/in-his-steps/.

Sheldon, Charles M. *In His Steps, Public Domain. What Saith the Scripture?* https://www.whatsaiththescripture.com/Text.Only/pdfs/In.His.Steps.Text.pdf. 14-15.

"Should we ban boxing?" *BMJ.* http://www.bmj.com/content/352/bmj.i389 (accessed January 3, 2018).

Sim, Alison. *Pleasures and Pastimes in Tudor England.* Gloucestershire: Stroud, 1999.

Simers, T.J. "The Life of a UFC Wife: The Modern Gladiators Do Battle, You Feel the Pain." *The New Ledger: Los Angeles Times,* July 2009.

Smith, Michael David. "UFC President Dana White: 'I Consider John McCain the Guy Who

Started the UFC.'" *MMA Fighting.* https://www.mmafighting.com/2008/06/22/ufc-president-dana-white-i-consider-john-mccain-the-guy-who-st (accessed August 9, 2017).

Smith, Michael David. "UFC 94 Video: B.J. Penn Tells Georges St. Pierre, 'I'm Going to Try to Kill You.'" *MMA Fighting.* http://www.mmafighting.com/2009/01/07/ufc-94-video-b-j-penn-tells-georges-st-pierre-im-going-to (accessed August 23, 2017).

Spickard, Paul R. et al., *A Global History of Christians: How Everyday Believers Experienced Their World.* Grand Rapids Michigan: Baker Academics, 1994. 44.

Sweet, Leonard. *11: Indispensable Relationships You Can't Be Without.* Colorado Springs: David C. Cook Publishing, 2012. 32.

Tertullian. "Spectacles." *Disciplinary, Moral and Ascetical Works* in *The Fathers of the Church.*

Trans. R. Arbesmann et al., vol. 40. New York: Fathers of the Church, 1959, 93.

Tertullian. *The Shows* or *De Spectaculis.* Chapter 3. http://www.tertullian.org/anf/anf03/anf03-09.htm#P905_359143 (accessed January 9, 2018).

Theophilus. *Ante-Nicene Fathers.* Christian Classics Ethereal Library, 2:116. http://www.ccel.org/ccel/schaff/anf02.iv.ii.iii.xv.html (accessed August 23, 2017.

Thorman, Joel. "Eric Winston: Fans cheering Matt Cassel's injury are 'sickening.'" *Arrowhead Pride.* https://www.arrowheadpride.com/2012/10/7/3470224/eric-winston-quotes-matt-cassel-injury-fans-cheering (accessed January 3, 2018).

Thrasher, Christopher David. *Fight Sports and American Masculinity: Salvation in Violence from 1609 to the Present.* North Carolina: McFarland & Company, Inc., 2015. 22.

Trotter, Jim. "Depression Prevalent in Ex-players." *ESPN.* http://www.espn.com/nfl/story/_/page/hotread150225/depression-suicide-raise-issue-mental-health-former-nfl-players (accessed August 28, 2017).

Visser, Josh. *CTV.ca News Staff,* July 11, 2009.

Walton, John. "The Four Kingdoms of Daniel." *JETS* 29/1 (March 1986) 25-36. http://www.etsjets.org/files/JETS-PDFs/29/29-1/29-1-pp025-036_JETS.pdf (accessed August 28, 2017).

Wells, Jonathan. "Knight fights: Inside the strange and savage world of medieval MMA." *The Telegraph.* http://www.telegraph.co.uk/men/the-filter/knight-fights-inside-the-strange-and-savage-world-of-medieval-mm   (accessed January 9, 2018).

Wiedemann, T. *Emperors and Gladiators.* London and New York: Routledge, 1992. 94-146.

Wills, Garry. "Bloodlust and the Superbowl." *New York Review Daily.* http://www.nybooks.com/daily/2011/02/04/blood-lust-and-super-bowl (accessed August 28, 2017).

Wills, Garry. "Blood Lust and the Super Bowl." *The New York Review of Books.* http://www.nybooks.com/blogs/nyrblog/2011/feb/04/blood-lust-and-super-bowl (accessed April 27, 2016).

"WMA Statement on Boxing," *World Medical Association,* https://www.wma.net/policies-post/wma-statement-on-boxing (accessed December 3, 2018).

Zezima, Katie. "How Teddy Roosevelt helped save football." *Washington Post.* https://www.washingtonpost.com/news/the-fix/wp/2014/05/29/teddy-roosevelt-helped-save-football-with-a-white-house-meeting-in-1905/?utm_term=.e56cb6933679 (accessed July 11, 2017).

For more information about
Trent Herbert
and

Gladiators Arising
please visit:

www.trentherbert.com

For more information about
AMBASSADOR INTERNATIONAL
please visit:

www.ambassador-international.com
@AmbassadorIntl
www.facebook.com/AmbassadorIntl

*Thank you for reading this book. Please consider leaving us a
review on your social media, favorite retailer's website,
Goodreads or Bookbub, or our website.*